Love Poetry

"How Do I Love Thee?"

Titles in the Pure Poetry series:

Beauty Poetry: "She Walks in Beauty"

ISBN 978-0-7660-4243-8

Death Poetry: "Death, Be Not Proud"

ISBN 978-0-7660-4257-5

Love Poetry: "How Do I Love Thee?"

ISBN 978-0-7660-4284-1

Nature Poetry: "Make Me a Picture of the Sun"

ISBN 978-0-7660-4244-5

Pure Poetry

Love Poetry

"How Do I Love Thee?"

Paula
Johanson

Enslow Publishers, Inc.
40 Industrial Road
Box 398
Berkeley Heights, NJ 07922
USA
http://www.enslow.com

Library of Congress Cataloging-in-Publication Data

Johanson, Paula.

   Love Poetry : "How Do I Love Thee?" / Paula Johanson.

     pages cm. — (Pure Poetry)

   Includes bibliographical references and index.

   Summary: "Explores love-themed poetry, including famous American and European
poets and their poems, as well as literary criticism, poetic technique, explication, and
prompts for further study"— Provided by publisher.

   ISBN 978-0-7660-4284-1

   1. Love poetry—History and criticism—Juvenile literature. 2. Poetry—Authorship—
Juvenile literature. I. Title.

   PN1076.J64 2014

   809.1'93543—dc23   2013014563

Future editions:

Paperback ISBN: 978-1-4644-0511-2

EPUB ISBN: 978-1-4645-1264-3

Single-User PDF ISBN: 978-1-4646-1264-0

Multi-User PDF ISBN: 978-0-7660-5896-5

Printed in the United States of America

112013 Lake Book Manufacturing, Inc., Melrose Park, IL

10 9 8 7 6 5 4 3 2 1

To Our Readers: We have done our best to make sure all Internet addresses in this book were
active and appropriate when we went to press. However, the author and the publisher have
no control over and assume no liability for the material available on those Internet sites or
on other Web sites they may link to. Any comments or suggestions can be sent by e-mail to
comments@enslow.com or to the address on the back cover.

♻ Enslow Publishers, Inc., is committed to printing our books on recycled paper. The paper
in every book contains 10% to 30% post-consumer waste (PCW). The cover board on the
outside of each book contains 100% PCW. Our goal is to do our part to help young people
and the environment too!

Photo and Illustration Credits: Library of Congress, pp. 28, 43, 63, 73, 101; Photos.
com/©Thinkstock, p. 51; Reproduced from the *Dictionary of American Portraits,* published by
Dover Publications, Inc., in 1967, p. 89.

Cover Illustration: Shutterstock.com.

Contents

Dedicated to my colleagues Sarah Milligan and Iain Higgins, whose discussions helped me shape this book.

Have you reckon'd a thousand acres much? have you reckon'd the earth much?
Have you practis'd so long to learn to read?
Have you felt so proud to get at the meaning of poems?
—Walt Whitman

Introduction

Of all writing, love poetry excites the strongest response in readers—a strong sense of self-identifying with the poet and the poet's emotion. Even when we who are reading the poem have not had for ourselves that all-consuming love, we as readers learn to recognize it—and to covet it for our own. We are taught to hope for this kind of love and to judge our loves by comparison with great love poetry.

There are many words for love in Latin, and some of them are used in English as well. *Filias* is the love for family members, which in English is called *filial love*. It's the love that Cordelia had for her father King Lear, as told in one of the many Shakespeare plays written in blank verse—a kind of poetry without rhyme except for a pair of rhymed lines at the end of each scene of the play.

Caritas is the caring sort of love that one can have for everyone, and it is the root of our English words *charity* and *caring*. *Agape* is similar to *caritas*, but it is used by Christians to name the love they feel for their fellow Christians. This love can have strong passions that are pure, and it has led to the poetry of hymns and sacred ceremonies.

Eros is the name for romantic and sexual love and from it comes the English word *erotic*. *Romance* is another word with deep roots. As a noun, it's that feeling of excitement and mystery associated with love. As a verb, *romance* has become a synonym for courting, or coaxing, a response from one's beloved. The word *romance* as it's used in English derives not so much from the city of Rome as from the Old French word *roman,* for a story written in the vernacular— in a plain, local language instead of the formal writing that was properly done in Latin. To be romancing someone, or to feel a sense of romance, is to be telling the story of love, in the plain language from the heart.

It's sometimes easier for readers in the twenty-first century to read love poetry written in plain language instead of artful constructions in fancy talk. That's one reason for the enduring popularity of modern love songs. Singer and songwriter Bob Dylan wrote of a complicated yet renewed love affair in his long ballad, "Tangled Up in Blue." At the center of the song, the narrator speaks of a woman opening up a book of poems written by an Italian poet. Every word felt true, as if the narrator wrote it himself, and seemed as bright and hot as burning coal.

That's how strongly some love poetry speaks to some readers—and that moment of connection is what poets are striving for when they write poetry about love. This book of Italian poems could be the work of Dante (1265–1321), in part because of the image of glowing "like burning coal," or Boccaccio (1313–1375). However, based on some interviews with Dylan, it is most likely a collection of Petrarch's (1304–1374) sonnets to his muse Laura. "In any event, Petrarch says that his first sight of Laura made him a poet," wrote literary critic Percy Hornstein in a commentary on Petrarch. "And his primary poetic theme is hopeless love, a spiritualized passion for the unattainable."[1]

All three of these poets from Renaissance Italy— Petrarch, Boccaccio, and Dante—wrote in the emerging language of their homeland as well as in Latin, which was the formal language used by proper, educated people. The idea of writing important things in the vernacular— in a plain, everyday local language—was new during the Renaissance. These poets wrote of love so strongly and eloquently that their poetry shaped the everyday language of their homeland.

By capturing the interests of readers across Europe, these poets shaped poetry in ways that have lasted for more than six hundred years, creating modern literature in European languages. While poetry made modern languages, what made these modern poets so able was love.

Because of this cultural heritage from the Italian Renaissance, it is still conventional hundreds of years later to think of love poetry as describing the true love a man has for a woman who is his soul mate. The woman is a muse, a mythical daughter of the gods, who inspires the poet to write. He describes her beauty in glowing terms, calling her the finest, fairest woman in the world. Or sometimes, the woman is a new world for him to discover. "O my America, my new-found-land," wrote John Donne (1572–1631) of his beloved, calling her, "My kingdom safeliest when with one man manned."[2] Certainly there are many fine poems of this kind, in English and other languages. But praising her matchless beauty is not the only way to praise one's beloved, as Shakespeare wrote eloquently. And the love of a man for his ideal woman is not the only inspiration for writing love poetry.

A love poem is usually thought to be expressing the personal love of one human being for another. In English poetry, as in most European poetry, the love is usually the love of a male poet for his ideal woman. But sometimes a poet is expressing love that is not specific or for one person. "I am he that aches with amorous love," wrote Walt Whitman in his life's major work, the poetry book *Leaves of Grass*. "Does the earth gravitate? does not all matter, aching, attract all matter?/So the body of me to all I meet or know."

A love poem can be intensely personal, and the love it describes can be intensely personal, even when the beloved is not a person. One of the strongest declarations of love in recent writing is the poem "Planet Earth" by P. K. Page (1916–2010). This poem is a *glosa,* a Spanish poetry form. In it, four stanzas are built on four lines of a different poem by another author, in this case Pablo Neruda (1904–1973). In Page's poem, she expands upon an image in Neruda's four lines about spreading out the skin of this planet and ironing it smooth with care. With a few plain words, Page makes it clear that what she has written is a poem of love for the whole earth and everything in it.

In both of their poems, Neruda and Page declare that the earth deserves to be loved—and that taking care of the world is a labor of love. Page expanded that image into a loving testimony of moving hands caring for the world, cleaning and tending it. When she read her poem aloud at Harbourfest Poetry Festival in Toronto, Canada, on Earth Day 2001, twenty thousand people wept. This kind of crowd response is more common at rock concerts and that is understandable. A large proportion of popular music is love poetry with music to support it.

Sometimes love seems to come out of nowhere. "Why must we love where the lightning strikes, and not where we choose?" wrote Theodore Sturgeon (1918–1985) at the end of a story in his collection *A Saucer of Loneliness.* "But I'm glad it's you, little prince. I'm glad it's you."

The act of falling in love can be quite sudden, and it's a common theme for love poetry. Much of this kind of love poetry describes the beloved's appearance and charm. But while "surface appearance is important for the act of *falling* in love, it is largely trivial for the state of *being* in love," stated scholar Dick Jenssen, when writing about Sturgeon.[3] Jenssen is not the only commentator to notice that many people fall in love for superficial reasons of lust and affection. It's only when the lover knows the beloved well that the charm wears off. Only the extremely lucky find that they are actually in love with a real person, says Jenssen, ". . . not the surface, which usually is still erotically arousing—but with their person, their inner core, their very soul. In short *we fall in love with the form, but are in love with the content*—it is the package which attracts, but it is what is inside the package which creates our love." As Jenssen adds wryly, this idea can be found in literature of quality, but it is not common in everyday, popular genres of writing.

In Thomas Moore's (1779–1852) best-known poem, "Believe Me, If All These Endearing Young Charms," Moore states that if his lover's youthful beauty fades, he would still have the same love for her. "This is what *real* love is all about," scholar Dick Jenssen writes. "Even if the object of our love changes physically, we still love them because their innermost being is unchanged. The ravages of time will not, cannot, if our love is true, make our love diminish, but will cause it to grow, vaster than empires and yet more slow."

Love doesn't always strike like lightning, unmistakable and undeniable. For some poets, the love they are describing is a search rather than a sudden revelation, and it is more gradual or intellectual than an emotional instant. As a writer working alone most of her days, Emily Dickinson took on writing about love for many reasons, instead of crabbing about things she hated. In her poem numbered XXII from her posthumous collected works, she explained that a lifetime would not be enough time to finish hating:

I had no time to hate, because
The grave would hinder me,
And life was not so ample I
Could finish enmity.

Nor had I time to love; but since
Some industry must be,
The little toil of love, I thought,
Was large enough for me.

Toil is hard work, but for Dickinson, learning to love and to write about love was not hard work. She felt she ought to do something worthwhile with her life, and this was enough of a challenge to keep her busy for a lifetime.

Writing about love has certainly challenged other poets, some only for the length of time it took to compose a short verse. Many poets found that decades weren't enough time to write everything they learned about love. Dante wrote thousands of verses on the Bible's themes of Heaven, Hell, and Redemption, inspired by the love he felt for his ideal woman, Beatrice. As Dante wrote, he believed the spirit of his beloved was guiding him through visions of heaven and hell. For this Italian poet, love was a grand thing that transcended death and eternity and could redeem the world. Petrarch wrote and rewrote sonnets and other poems, inspired by his love for Laura. His 366 poems—one for every day of the year, even in a leap year—are among the most polished and perfected works of Western European writing.

There are also simpler and more direct poems, written by more recent writers in the United States and around the world. "Little you know the subtle electric fire that for your sake is playing within me," wrote Walt Whitman in one of the shortest poems from his book *Leaves of Grass,* in an attempt to describe feelings of warm attraction.

The greeting card industry supports itself on most people's belief that as ordinary people, we might not have the ability to write the proper words, coherent and evocative, for our own readers. But coherence is not always a necessary element of love poetry. See "anyone lived in a pretty how town" by E. E. Cummings for an incoherent example of love poetry. As a poet, Cummings tried to write poems with images that challenged the reader's expectations for how words ought to fit together.

Cummings wrote verses that looked like word salad. Words are in unexpected order. Syntax and punctuation are not necessary in Cummings's kind of poetry. What is necessary in love poetry is to evoke feeling—a response in the reader to the love being expressed by the poet.

The poems analyzed in this book are some of the best love poetry and some that are easiest for readers to approach and discuss. All of them are poems that evoke feelings—sometimes unexpected feelings—in response to these carefully crafted words. While the careful polishing and revising done by these poets show more in some of these poems than in others, all of them were made to speak of love.

1

"Westron Wynde"
Anonymous

Ballads and love songs are a good place to begin a study of love poems. There's no way to be sure when people first began to sing songs. But in the English language, people have been singing ballads and songs about love from the beginnings of our language as Old English around the fifth century. Old English is another name for the Anglo-Saxon language used by invaders of the British Isles who came from the area that is now northern Germany.

By the twelfth century, Old English was changing into what is now called Middle English. As songs were shared from person to person, and ballads were sung to tell stories in a consistent rhythm, songs became part of the changes that were happening in the English language. Love was a theme for many of these songs, whether the love was honored or betrayed, or whether it was the love of loyalty or of romance. One song in particular is remembered as one of the first songs in English that was written down, "Westron Wynde." Beginning in the fourteenth century, it was popularly shared by word of mouth for about two hundred years throughout England before being written down by men composing music for church services.

Summary

The narrator in this poem speaks first to the West Wind, asking when will the wind blow, perhaps to bring a light rain with it, or perhaps because the rain is falling. Then the narrator speaks to Christ, wishing to be holding his beloved in bed.

This four-line poem seems to be the first verse of a longer song, but the other verses, if any, have been lost. In this poem, the speaker is not identified by name or place. There is no hint of gender, but it is common to think of this narrator as a man because he seems to be outdoors, perhaps working or on guard duty.

It's unclear why the West Wind is being asked to blow, or whether the narrator is asking for rain or the rain is being acknowledged as continuing to fall. Perhaps it is winter and a mild wind would be welcome, bringing a light rain to melt the snow. The speaker could be a soldier patrolling on watch, wishing for the steady rain to be blown away. Another reading is that the narrator is a farmer hoping for

Westron Wynde

Westron wynde, when wyll thou blow,
The smalle rayne downe can rayne.
Cryst, yf my louve wer in my armes
And I in my bedde agayne!

In modern spelling, the poem reads:

Western wind, when will you blow,
The small rain down can rain.
Christ, if my love were in my arms
And I in my bed again!

a gentle rain to water the crops. Since the speaker loves someone who cannot be with him now, this is a classic love poem of yearning for the unattainable beloved.

The speaker in this poem addresses both the West Wind and Christ, an odd combination that deserves more discussion. Use of the word "thou" is rare in modern English; it means "you" when speaking informally to one person, or to someone you know well. Except among Quakers, in the twenty-first century "thou" is used only in some prayers to God.

The Tune

This short quatrain, or verse of four lines, was a song already old when it was written down in the early sixteenth century. The tune can be guessed by working backward from church music, which used the tune of "Westron Wynde" for the main theme. It's assumed that this song was well known for perhaps a hundred or two hundred years before it was written down. Though there were few people in England who could read and write during the fourteenth and fifteenth centuries, many people loved to sing. People would listen to songs about interesting stories and share them with friends and neighbors. Sometimes new words would be put to an old tune, or new versions of a story would be told in verse.

The tune for "Westron Wynde" was probably as familiar to people in the fifteenth and sixteenth centuries as the "Alphabet Song" is to modern readers. The original

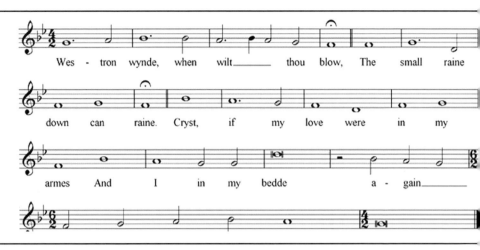

A music sheet with the tune for "Westron Wynde."

composer of the "Westron Wynde" words to this tune is unknown. The person who invented the tune might also have made up the words for this verse, but there is no way to know anything about the other verses. It's possible that the song originally had other verses that told a complete story from beginning to end, and everyone who heard the tune in the sixteenth century would remember the story.

Word Choice

There are only twenty-six words in this short fragment of what was probably a longer song. In his literary column in the *Globe and Mail* newspaper in 2001, Fraser Sutherland pointed out that all but one of this poem's words have their roots in Old English and Anglo-Saxon. The exception is

"Christ," which came to English from Latin and Greek with Christian missionaries.

There are only short words in this poem, too. Two dozen of these twenty-six words have only one syllable. The longest word has only seven letters. The result is that the lines feel lean and plain, not ornamental and decorated. The words are easy to pronounce quickly and cleanly. The verse is short, direct, and to the point.

There have been many versions of this short verse written throughout the centuries as it has appeared in poetry collections. Some versions insert extra syllables, such as an "O!" at the beginning, or replacing the word *Christ* with a less intense interjection. Replacing the word *Christ* can make a huge difference in how the poem is understood.

If the word *Christ* is being used here as just a curse word for emphasis, it could easily be replaced with any other short, sharp word that is used for expressing frustration and anger. Then the last two lines would be the grumbling complaint of a lustful soldier or tired farmer who wants to go back to bed. Or is the word *Christ* being used as a prayer? If so, why was the West Wind being addressed in the same way? The poet has written an apostrophe, addressing both the West Wind as an element of the natural world and Christ as part of the Holy Trinity of God. That's an interesting combination, considering it came from a time when pagan beliefs still existed among the common people of England.

Clearly, the poet (or at least the narrator) is a Christian, or is supposed to be one, even though he addresses the West Wind as well as Christ. It is just as clear that the narrator is not supposed to be a priest, as he has a lover. And since the beloved is not named as a wife, there are lingering questions. Is the beloved a wife or not? If not, why is the narrator not married to the beloved? Is the beloved a woman or a man? Why are the lovers apart? Why is the narrator not at home in bed?

Ballad Format

Written in ballad format, this short verse has lines that are mostly in iambic beats—an unstressed syllable followed by a stressed syllable. There are a few extra unstressed syllables and a missing unstressed syllable or two, so the pattern is not perfectly regular. But the number of stresses in each line is that of a format commonly used in ballads: four stresses in the first line, followed by three stresses in the second line. The pattern repeats for four stresses in the third line, followed by three stresses in the fourth.

The end of the second line rhymes with the end of the fourth line. Rhyme patterns are noted by writing a letter for each line, starting with *a* for the first line and using a new letter of the alphabet for each line that doesn't rhyme with an earlier line. For example, "Westron Wynde" has the rhyme pattern *abcb*.

Soldier Poem

This little poem has had echoes in other poetry through the years. W. H. Auden was drawing on the same source when he wrote "Roman Wall Blues" from the viewpoint of a Roman soldier at Hadrian's Wall in conquered Britain. The lines of Auden's poem are usually written in dactyls—a stressed syllable followed by two unstressed syllables—rather than in iambic meter. The dactyl meter is not perfectly regular, as sometimes there's an unstressed beat out of place, which is common in ballad format. The four short lines of "Westron Wynde" take about as long to read aloud as a rhymed couplet from "Roman Wall Blues."

It was sensible for Auden to start with this quatrain when composing his series of couplets, as some scholars think that "Westron Wynde" was a fragment of a military song from medieval times. Traditional folk songs are often the inspiration for new compositions with similar themes and images. "Westron Wynde" was also the inspiration for Bob Dylan's song "If Today Were Not an Endless Highway" according to some reviewers.

Ballad format is also known as common meter or common measure. The result of common use of this pattern is that lyrics of one song can be sung to the tune of another. Like military songs, "Westron Wynde" is easy to read aloud to the rhythm of marching. In fact, it can be sung to tunes as varied as some church hymns such as "Amazing Grace," the ballad "Barbara Allen," a bawdy military marching song such as "North Atlantic Squadron," and the Canadian patriotic song "The Maple Leaf Forever."

A Steady Chant

The first known written version of "Westron Wynde" appeared in a book written around 1530 in England. The book held mainly keyboard music for singing masses in four parts. A Mass is a Christian church service during which the sacraments of bread and wine are consecrated for communion.

Starting around A.D. 900, many composers who wrote sacred music to be sung in church services would write masses with a *cantus firmus,* which is a tune chanted by one voice as the main theme. The three other parts would be more decorative embellishments around the main tune, in which many notes would be held for a long time. It became popular on the European continent for some composers to write the sacred text of the church service so that it might be sung to a familiar melody from a secular song. Often the vernacular, or the local language of the common people, was used for singing the lyrics of love poetry above a voice chanting the church service in Latin. The practice lasted until the seventeenth century.

The tune for "Westron Wynde" was the first secular song used by an English composer for this purpose. First to use it was sixteenth-century composer John Tavener in one of his most influential works still performed today. One musical commentator wrote of Tavener's "switching between voices in a series of polyphonic [many voices] variations. . . . Each voice gives us a new perspective on the melody."[1] The Tudor kings of England would have listened to this music.

Tavener's Mass was soon followed by others written by John Sheppard and Christopher Tye. The tune of "Westron Wynde" became a *cantus firmus* when each of these men was composing masses to be sung at their sponsoring cathedrals. A similar technique was used by modern music artists to compose the songs recorded on Enigma's 1991 album *MCMXC a.D.*, which combined Gregorian chant and suggestive lyrics with synthesized beats, flutes, and rain forest sounds. "This is a holy package with a seamy underbelly," wrote one reviewer.[2] A little of the intensity of that combination of sacred and profane is probably what the church composers were looking for when they used "Westron Wynde" as a *cantus firmus.*

Further Study Questions

1. Is the narrator of the poem a man or a woman? Why do you think so?

2. Is it stealing when a composer writes music to be performed in public using the tune of an anonymous folk song?

3. If "Westron Wynde" is all that is left of a longer song, compose another verse that would be suitable for the song.

4. Does it matter to you that the name of this poet is no longer remembered? Do poems matter more to you when you know who has written them and who was the subject of the poet's story? Who is this anonymous poet to you—is this a specific person who has been forgotten or could it be anyone?

5. What are some other traditional poems or songs or hymns that have been used by composers to make great pieces of music? If you were writing a piece of music to perform, what traditional song might you use?

2

"Sonnet 130"
William Shakespeare
(1564–1616)

William Shakespeare was a man of common birth, born in Stratford, England, who had no more than a "grammar school" education—about the equivalent of a modern elementary school but with the addition of some studies in Latin and the classic works of Roman writers.

He rose above these humble beginnings, first as a tutor and then as a writer. While still a young man, Shakespeare left his wife and children in Stratford to pursue a career in London, writing plays in blank verse for production in public theaters. He returned home at intervals before retiring in Stratford.

William Shakespeare

When the poem, later known as "Sonnet 130," was written around 1595, Shakespeare was in his mid-thirties. Much of England was gripped by an envy of the prosperity that the Renaissance had already brought to Italy. Through merchant ships sailing the known parts of the world, scientific advances allowing better navigation and improved fabric weaving, and the construction of prosperous cities with brilliant architecture and fine artworks, Italy had experienced a cultural and intellectual revival.

The Renaissance came later to England than to Italy and France, around 1485. English intellectuals felt this delay keenly and worked to enrich and renew their country's literature and culture. While scientists worked busily to make new discoveries and inventions, writers also worked to bring a renaissance to English literature, such as the one Dante and Petrarch had brought to Italy some two hundred years earlier.

Shakespeare was one of many writers and poets who were able to earn a living by writing plays and through financial support from a noble sponsor. He enjoyed moderate acclaim and some financial success in his lifetime, and his reputation has grown in the centuries since his death so that now he has become the most celebrated of the English poets and playwrights.

Sonnet 130

My mistress' eyes are nothing like the sun;
Coral is far more red than her lips' red;
If snow be white, why then her breasts are dun*;
If hairs be wires, black wires grow on her head;
I have seen roses damasked*, red and white,
But no such roses see I in her cheeks;
And in some perfumes is there more delight
Than in the breath that from my mistress reeks.
I love to hear her speak, yet well I know
That music hath a far more pleasing sound;
I grant I never saw a goddess go—
My mistress when she walks treads on the ground:
   And yet, by heaven, I think my love as rare
   As any she belied with false compare.

*dun: brown

*damasked: decorated in contrasting colors like damask fabric

Shakespeare's Sonnet Sequence

The speaker in the poem says that his mistress is not beautiful in the exaggerated ways that other poets describe their beloveds. He does love her and thinks his love is as fine as any unrealistic images in other poems.

It was the convention for sonnet sequences, such as those written by Petrarch and later Shakespeare, to describe courtly love, notes scholar Sarah Milligan, "in which a lowborn poet expresses his unrequited love for a noble woman whom he can never possess because she is 'absent, unattainable or dead.'"[1]

The Italian sonnet (meaning "little song") form that Petrarch made popular consisted of an octave of eight lines and a sestet of six lines. There would be at the ninth line a turn, or volta, in the argument or mood. The octave would have an end rhyme scheme of *abbaabba*, and the sestet would have the pattern *cdecde* or *cdcdcd*. In English sonnets, Shakespeare made popular a different rhyme scheme of three quatrains with a couplet at the end: *abab cdcd efef gg*. In this pattern, the volta traditionally occurred in the final rhyming couplet.

The volta in a sonnet is as important a moment as the *kake kotoba* word in Japanese haiku poetry, which works as a pivot point or hinge for the poem and where the focus of the poem has a meaningful shift. By using a volta in this sonnet, the poet is able to set up and then complete a complicated turn of thought.

Why would Shakespeare choose a foreign language's form for poetry when English was coming into its own? One of his reasons was the same as why he set many of his plays in Verona and other Italian locations—because it was fashionable then to imitate the successes of Italian culture. Another reason was the lasting appeal of the sonnet as perfected by Petrarch, which "comes from the combination of form and content," according to literary historian Percy Hornstein.

Petrarch is permanently in the center of the stage, exploring indefatigably all the delicate phenomena of his emotions. His sentiments come from the discord between the senses and the soul, the flesh and the spirit, the sensuality of his love and a mystic acceptance of its spirituality. No wonder the poems swept Europe and immortalized their author. Their mood, imagery, and rhyme scheme dominated literary circles for centuries.[2]

It's really no surprise that Shakespeare wrote many sonnets. What is surprising is how Shakespeare reverses some of the Petrarchan conventions. In this sonnet, the poet describes his beloved's actual appearance instead of presenting an idealized or unrealistic picture of her. By mentioning her lips and breasts, the poet shows he has an erotic love for her, not the courtly love of a distant admirer. When the poet states that this woman walks on the ground, he is emphasizing her human qualities rather than comparing her to an angel or goddess.

There are also some unusual tricks in the rhymes of this poem. While the poet follows the then-current fashion of rhyming alternating lines (*abab, cdcd, efef*) in this sonnet, the words chosen for the rhymes are unexpected. Who would ever expect a poet to say that his woman's breasts are dun, a dull brown like an unremarkable workhorse, even though the word dun rhymes with sun? What sort of love poem rhymes cheeks with reeks? These words succeed as rhymes, but they also succeed at bringing a rough and robust attitude to these carefully crafted lines.

The speaker in this poem is not timid, limply praising an idle porcelain doll of a woman. Instead, he is a man of experience who is able to call a spade a spade. Is this love more real than most love poetry of that time because it is more realistic? The final couplet is completed by its rhyme. It suggests that the poet might have composed this poem after his beloved complained that he never wrote her a love poem as real poets do.

Describing His Mistress

It was fashionable for a poet to indulge in hyperbole, or exaggerated descriptions of his beloved as if she were a Greek goddess, with hair like gold and eyes blazing as bright as the sun. She would also be fair-skinned, and fair means not only smooth-skinned and pretty but pale because noble women would not have suntanned faces and hands from working outdoors. "The blazon is a Petrarchan convention of describing the features of the female beloved in hyperbolic terms," notes scholar Sarah Milligan, who also says Shakespeare uses parody to reject and mock this convention when he says that his mistress's eyes "are nothing like the sun."[3]

It is possible that Shakespeare was describing a real woman he knew who was not a blonde Englishwoman. Her hair is like black wires, her skin under her clothing is brown, her lips are not red, and her cheeks are not flushed red and white. Her eyes are dark, since they are "nothing like the sun." In a related poem, "Sonnet 132," he calls them black. This is a good description of a woman of African descent, or possibly a Gypsy woman of Romany descent.

Shakespeare's sonnets have many references to this Dark Lady, and "Sonnet 130" is not the only poem in which Shakespeare acknowledges that his mistress might not be perfect. Among his collected poems, sonnets 127 through 154 are considered his Dark Lady sonnets. In "Sonnet 131," the poet again addresses the Dark Lady, saying in the first lines: "Thou art as tyrannous, so as thou art,/As those whose beauties proudly make them cruel." And in the final couplet, he writes: "In nothing art thou black save in thy deeds,/And thence this slander, as I think, proceeds." These poems speak of a young man whom the poet loves as well but who has also been seduced by the Dark Lady.

They have formed a love triangle, as the poet complains in "Sonnet 134," saying: "Him have I lost; thou hast both him and me:/He pays the whole, and yet am I not free." In "Sonnet 144," the poet states baldly that

> Two loves I have of comfort and despair,
> Which like two spirits do suggest me still:
> The better angel is a man right fair,
> The worser spirit a woman colored ill.

As the sequence of Shakespeare's sonnets progresses, it becomes clear that the Dark Lady is a complicated character, and the poet both blesses and curses his relationship with her. "The poet is both attracted and repelled by the Dark Woman," wrote scholar Michael Best. "His language, though now difficult, is subtle, richly varied, and eloquent."[4] Shakespeare was writing in the King's English, the emerging dialect of his home district and London, but he did not limit himself to simple words in his poetry.

The Natural Order?

When Shakespeare was alive, there was no idea of equality between the sexes. In England, church leaders taught that the Bible said Adam was created before Eve and that Eve was created specifically to give comfort to Adam. In this worldview, woman was supposed to be subordinate to man. A woman was expected to obey first her father and then her husband when she married and to accept her lesser status.

Born Too Soon?

"I would to God Shakespeare had lived later, & promenaded in Broadway," wrote American novelist Herman Melville to a friend in 1849, some 233 years after Shakespeare died in 1616.

> *Not that I might have had the pleasure of leaving my card for him at the Astor, or made merry with him over a bowl of the fine Duyckinck punch; but that the muzzle which all men wore on their soul in the Elizabethan day, might not have intercepted Shakespeare's full articulations. For I hold it a verity, that even Shakespeare, was not a frank man to the uttermost. And, indeed, who in this intolerant universe is, or can be? But the Declaration of Independence makes a difference.*[5]

It wasn't Melville's wish merely to meet this most celebrated of writers at a fine hotel. He didn't want only to share a bowl of punch at a party hosted by Evert Duyckinck, who was the publisher of Edgar Allen Poe and, as the editor of the *Literary World* review of books, one of the leading men of the New York literary scene in the 1840s. Melville had a theory that if born in the United States after the American Revolution, Shakespeare might have written far more frankly than in his Elizabethan poetry. Other literary minds have similar opinions about early American poetry. In the first few centuries of American poetry, there was a strong sense of independence.

In those circumstances, it is remarkable that Shakespeare wrote of women who were competent and confident, not submissive. By writing of a Dark Lady, who had an active mind instead of a pale and idle beauty, Shakespeare was challenging what many people thought was the natural order of the world. "A dominant woman was unnatural, a symptom of disorder," observed scholar Michael Best on the *Internet Shakespeare* Web site. "The medieval church had inculcated a view of women that was split between the ideal of the Virgin Mary, and her fallible counterpart, Eve, or her anti-type, the Whore of Babylon. Unfortunately, the Virgin Mary was one of a kind, so there was often a general distrust of women; Renaissance and Medieval literature is often misogynistic."

It is understandable that most of the poetry published in English by poets born before 1800 was written by men. Before 1800, women did not usually receive as much formal education as men. Women made use of poetry in their homes, from humble cottages to fine houses, or in the seclusion of a nunnery. Poetry performed aloud for a wide audience, or published, was written by men. It was a cultural belief of the Anglo-Saxons and, for hundreds of years the English (unlike the British Celts they replaced), that women should not be allowed to display themselves in that way. Even in theaters where Shakespeare's plays were performed, until the late 1700s, male actors dressed as women and played all the female roles.

Of course, it is impossible to know how many male poets presented the work of their wives and family members as if it were their own. Many male poets after Shakespeare, such as John Milton or William Wordsworth, acknowledged that they relied on at least one female family member to take dictation or as a writing partner.

Shakespeare was stretching the bounds of what was considered the natural order for men and women when he dared to write verses about his Dark Lady and put other female characters who were his peers into his plays. "Sonnet 130" was a challenge to the social conventions of the time. Shakespeare was admired in spite of this poem and others that he wrote about the Dark Lady—not because of them. It took two centuries after his death for a female poet to rise to similar public acclaim.

Further Study Questions

1. Can you identify exactly where the volta occurs in this sonnet? How many words does the poet take to make this volta?

2. What is the one quality of his mistress that the narrator actually mentions in this poem that he loves?

3. What could be some reasons for the poet mentioning heaven in the second to last line of the poem?

4. In "Sonnet 130," how realistic is the description of the poet's beloved? Perhaps you can draw a sketch or make a picture that would look like her. Is the poet describing her more or less accurately than if he claimed to be dazzled by her bright eyes?

5. How is a volta in an English sonnet anything like a *kake kotoba* word, or hinge word, in a Japanese haiku poem? Compare the volta in this sonnet with a hinge word from a haiku and list some ways in which they are similar and different.

"How Do I Love Thee?"
Elizabeth Barrett Browning
(1806–1861)

At the time that she wrote this poem, Elizabeth Barrett was considered the finest female poet in England. More than a bit mysterious, she rarely left her father's house. Victorian female poets typically had modest female speakers in their poems. In this sonnet, she created an appropriately modest narrator but one who challenges convention by addressing her beloved as though she felt empowered.

After her marriage to poet Robert Browning, when this poem was published in her book *Sonnets From the Portuguese,* readers viewed Barrett's sonnets as the product of a romantic love story. Love sonnets were traditionally associated with a male poet's unrequited love for a noble woman who inspires him but whom he could never marry. However, in Barrett's sonnet sequence, the female speaker in her poems is inspired by her love of another male poet.

Elizabeth Barrett Browning

How Do I Love Thee? (Sonnet XLIII)

How do I love thee? Let me count the ways.
I love thee to the depth and breadth and height
My soul can reach, when feeling out of sight
For the ends of Being and ideal Grace.
I love thee to the level of every day's
Most quiet need, by sun and candle-light.
I love thee freely, as men strive for Right;
I love thee purely, as they turn from Praise.
I love thee with the passion put to use
In my old griefs, and with my childhood's faith.
I love thee with a love I seemed to lose
With my lost saints,—I love thee with the breath,
Smiles, tears, of all my life; and, if God choose,
I shall but love thee better after death.

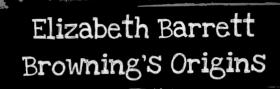

Elizabeth Barrett Browning's Origins

In 1806, Elizabeth Barrett was the first in her family to be born in England in more than two hundred years. The Barrett family owned sugar plantations in Jamaica, relying on slave labor. Elizabeth's father chose to raise his family in England and forbade any of his children to marry, apparently from fear that a dark-skinned grandchild would reveal his Creole origins.

Educated at home, Elizabeth was a bright student of the classics, who developed a lung ailment at fourteen. At fifteen, she suffered a spinal injury while saddling a pony. Bitterly opposed to slavery, Elizabeth endured her father's tyranny and her own ill health. The books of verse she wrote were met with increasing acclaim as she spent years rarely leaving her room.

Summary

The speaker in this poem lists many ways in which she loves her beloved. The list uses a technique called anaphora, in which the poet repeats words at the beginning of lines to keep the ideas organized in sequence. She loves as far as she can imagine her soul reaching, extending farther than can be seen. She loves on ordinary days also. She loves as people try to do what is right, and she loves without hope of being admired or gaining anything. She loves with the strong emotions that she used to have of grief and religious faith in childhood. Every breath and feeling she has is another way to love the beloved. The speaker breaks the pattern of anaphora only at the end of the poem, saying that if God allows her to love after death, she is confident that she will love her beloved even more.

The question "How do I love thee?" and answers in "Sonnet XLIII" sum up the many meanings of love that are contemplated through Barrett's sonnet series. "The sequence thus rewrites the Petrarchan tradition, but it does so while conversely upholding it," scholar Sarah Milligan writes. "The female speaker inhabits a male genre, maintaining and dismantling that genre simultaneously from within."[1]

As "Sonnet XLIII" progresses, the speaker's past is rewritten. "Old griefs" and "lost saints" are reinterpreted now that the narrator is declaring her love. The lost faith of her childhood is renewed when she loves. By embracing her past, she is able to love freely and strive to do right in the future. The narrator is shown to be a capable person, who recognizes that she is subject to God's will and to death. It is significant that the final word of the poem is "death."

A Frail Speaker

Some readers consider the narrator in "Sonnet XLIII" to be an invalid—a person who is too sick or disabled to function—because this character is an autobiographical character representing Barrett herself. That is an oversimplification, which undermines the poet's goals in constructing her sonnet sequence. "While the Sonnets were initially read as a sentimental artifact of the Brownings' famous romance," as scholar Sarah Milligan notes, "feminist scholars in the 1970s and 1980s reclaimed the text and considered its subversion of the gendered roles of male poet and female muse."

Milligan argues that the speaker in Barrett's sonnets does not just happen to be an invalid, but that the fact she is an invalid should be crucial to understanding the entire sonnet sequence. Instead of reading the sonnets as a purely autobiographical statement by Barrett, Milligan considers "that the speaker of the Sonnets performs her invalidity in a highly self-conscious fashion and, in doing so, participates in the cult of poetic celebrity." If so, then by using an invalid for a narrator, the poet is evoking and rewriting a larger tradition of sonnet writing, as well as revising the definition of an invalid in the Victorian era.

The primary way that Barrett revises the image of a frail, invalid poet is by depicting the speaker in her poem as a lover who is strong and effective in love, though still physically weak. Barrett uses verbs followed by modifying or adverbial phrases, and the images in these phrases are meant to evoke vivid feelings rather than sights or sounds. The speaker's soul is described as reaching as far as her imagination and is not limited by her body's weakness. The speaker has strong passions, such as grief and faith, which she has mastered as an adult. By loving her beloved, the speaker has integrated her past and memories together with her hopes for the future and has accepted that she is subject to God who will choose her future.

Rebuilding the Sonnet

"Sonnet XLIII" is a good example of the structure of the poems written by Barrett in her sonnet series. Her subject matter and rhyme scheme are compatible with the Italian sonnet form made popular by Petrarch. Though the lines of this poem meet the rhyme scheme of *abbaabba cdcdcd*, the lines do not form an octave and a sestet, divided by a volta. Instead, in a deviation from the Italian form that is typical of Barrett's sonnets, there is more than one volta within this poem. The final volta in "Sonnet XLIII" occurs during the last two lines, as in an English sonnet by Shakespeare, when Barrett writes her last sentence, which is extended over three lines:

> . . . *I love thee with the breath,*
> *Smiles, tears, of all my life; and, if God choose,*
> *I shall but love thee better after death.*

The volta comes at the semicolon, where the speaker's statement changes from a definite statement of how she loves the beloved to a conditional statement of how she will love him after death, *if* permitted by God.

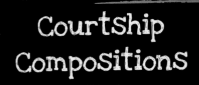

Courtship Compositions

When emerging poet Robert Browning was introduced to Elizabeth Barrett in 1845, they began an extraordinary courtship kept secret from her father. During twenty months, they exchanged nearly six hundred letters. When they eloped in 1846, Barrett left her sickroom behind.

In Italy, when Browning began to find his own writing success and the couple's son was born, Barrett gave him a sonnet series that she had written during their courtship. It was published under the title *Sonnets From the Portuguese*. Their son published his parents' correspondence after their deaths. Among many readers and critics, the story of their courting has taken attention away from Barrett's sonnets and other writing. As one student scholar observed, "The letters are the communication between two people and the sonnets are the communication of one woman trying to articulate love."[2]

In addition, these lines are one of the three times in this sonnet that Barrett uses enjambment to extend her phrasing from one line to the next. She uses this technique between the second and third lines, the fifth and sixth lines, and the twelfth and thirteenth lines. Enjambment is when the verb in a phrase is on a different line from its subject or its object. When reading a poem, it often seems natural to put the end of a phrase at the end of a line. There might be a period or a comma at the end of a line, but it is not required. When

Barrett puts the subject and verb of line twelve ("I love") but extends part of the object of the verb ("thee with the breath, smiles, tears, of all my life") over onto the next line, her thought is not finished at the end of line twelve. This device pulls the reader immediately onward to the next line without pause. The poet is working within the rhyming pattern but has some freedom within that pattern. Petrarch did not commonly use enjambment.

Readers should note that Barrett's "adherence to the formal limitations of the sonnet represents a desire to participate in the sonnet tradition in a meaningful way," as Milligan observes. However, she had another desire as well. "[T]he deviance from those same limitations reveals a simultaneous intention to challenge and rewrite that form." Barrett is not just a slave to structure.

It is too simple to read "Sonnet XLIII" as the poet's personal declaration of love for the man she had chosen to marry. The poems in this series appear to be personal statements but far from being casually written, they are sonnets—one of the most demanding poetic forms. The restrictions and aesthetic demands of sonnets are a way to construct artificially a display of the emotions that the poet intends to display. Barrett was aware of how the public perceived her—as poet, invalid, and unmarried woman—and as she constructed the sonnets that she was contributing to the public image of herself.

Throughout the sonnet sequence, the poet can be seen setting up and dismantling the reader's expectations. She replaces the expected male voice with a female voice. Instead of a lovesick poet, the poet is actually an invalid. Instead of an absent woman as a muse for inspiration, another poet inspires the speaker. As Barrett's sonnet sequence progresses, there is movement toward a marriage of equal partners, which is a different conclusion from the usual unrequited love for the unattainable in Petrarchan sonnets.

Further Study Questions

1. How is the repeated phrase "I love thee" made newly meaningful instead of merely repetitive?

2. Why does line 7 say "as men strive for right?" Does the poet mean that it is only males who strive to do what is right?

3. What clues can you find to suggest the speaker is older than a young woman in her teenage years?

4. How does the narrator in "Sonnet XLIII" seem to be proud and capable, while at the same time modest?

5. Is there any obvious sign in this particular poem to make a present-day reader understand that the poet or the narrator is a woman? What difference would it make if the narrator were a man? Would any changes to the words be necessary to make the speaker in this poem be a male person?

4

"My Last Duchess" Robert Browning (1812–1889)

In 1845, when a twenty-month-long courtship by correspondence began between poets Elizabeth Barrett and Robert Browning, Barrett was already considered England's greatest living female poet. Browning, though only six years younger, was still struggling to achieve success as a poet. His second book, *Sordello,* took him seven years to write. It was by some accounts a complete failure, selling only one copy from the first print run in 1840—not even his mother or his patrons bought copies. From his second book, Browning gained only a "reputation of being the most pretentious and abstruse poet in England," observed scholar Sarah Milligan, "a stereotype that plagued him for at least two decades."[1]

In courting Elizabeth Barrett, Browning found his artistic center. With their marriage in 1846, he

gained confidence that gradually transformed his poetry—
and in particular, critical opinions of it—into much more
popular and praised verses. Eventually, his reputation grew
to match hers and continued to do so after their deaths
until the emergence of feminist literary theory brought
renewed interpretations of Barrett's poetry. Because of that
love story enriching his career, it's significant that "My Last
Duchess" is one of the most well-remembered poems by
Browning, as it is a poem describing very different forms of
love from his own marriage.

Set during the late Renaissance in Italy, this poem
is the words of a duke as he is giving the emissary of his
prospective second wife a tour of his home and the works
of art he has collected. The duke draws aside a curtain to
reveal a portrait of his
late wife; together he
and his visitor look
at the painting. The
duke describes his
first wife's nature,
which he felt was
flawed. She enjoyed
and appreciated many
things but had no
special joy for him
alone. He gave orders
that suppressed all her

Robert Browning

My Last Duchess

Ferrara

That's my last Duchess painted on the wall,
Looking as if she were alive. I call
That piece a wonder, now: Frà* Pandolf's hands
Worked busily a day, and there she stands.
Will't please you sit and look at her? I said
"Frà Pandolf" by design, for never read
Strangers like you that pictured countenance*,
The depth and passion of its earnest glance,
But to myself they turned (since none puts by
The curtain I have drawn for you, but I)
And seemed as they would ask me, if they durst,
How such a glance came there; so, not the first
Are you to turn and ask thus. Sir, 'twas not
Her husband's presence only, called that spot
Of joy into the Duchess' cheek: perhaps
Frà Pandolf chanced to say "Her mantle* laps
Over my lady's wrist too much," or "Paint
Must never hope to reproduce the faint
Half-flush that dies along her throat": such stuff
Was courtesy, she thought, and cause enough
For calling up that spot of joy. She had
A heart—how shall I say?—too soon made glad,
Too easily impressed; she liked whate'er
She looked on, and her looks went everywhere.
Sir, 'twas all one! My favor at her breast,
The dropping of the daylight in the West,
The bough of cherries some officious fool
Broke in the orchard for her, the white mule
She rode with round the terrace—all and each

Would draw from her alike the approving speech,
Or blush, at least. She thanked men,—good! but thanked
Somehow—I know not how—as if she ranked
My gift of a nine-hundred-years-old name
With anybody's gift. Who'd stoop to blame
This sort of trifling? Even had you skill
In speech—(which I have not)—to make your will
Quite clear to such an one, and say, "Just this
Or that in you disgusts me; here you miss,
Or there exceed the mark"—and if she let
Herself be lessoned so, nor plainly set
Her wits to yours, forsooth, and made excuse,
—E'en then would be some stooping; and I choose
Never to stoop. Oh sir, she smiled, no doubt,
Whene'er I passed her; but who passed without
Much the same smile? This grew; I gave commands;
Then all smiles stopped together. There she stands
As if alive. Will't please you rise? We'll meet
The company below, then. I repeat,
The Count your master's known munificence*
Is ample warrant that no just pretence
Of mine for dowry will be disallowed;
Though his fair daughter's self, as I avowed
At starting, is my object. Nay, we'll go
Together down, sir. Notice Neptune, though,
Taming a sea-horse, thought a rarity,
Which Claus of Innsbruck cast in bronze for me!

*Frà: friar
*countenance: face
*mantle: cloak
*munificence: generosity

happiness, and now she is dead. The duke then seems to return to an earlier conversation concerning arrangements for his planned wedding. In passing, he points out another work of art he commissioned, a bronze statue of Neptune.

Three Forms of Love

In this poem, Browning uses a series of rhyming couplets written in iambic pentameter. An iamb is a unit of one unaccented syllable followed by an accented syllable. The root of pentameter, penta, means five, so there are five feet/ten syllables in a line written in iambic pentameter. Browning uses this popular poetry form to create not only a narrative that is a dramatic monologue but depictions of three forms of love. Each form of love is described briefly but evocatively.

First, and in most detail, Browning depicts the love felt by the "last duchess"—what a twenty-first century reader might call the "late duchess" or the duke's first wife, now dead. The love this woman felt was not specific but general. Her smile was bestowed on any pleasant person or thing around her. She did not reserve her joy, blushes, or attention for the duke only. She had, and showed, appreciation for all good things that came to her. This generous love is like that of the angels and saints. In Latin, this love is called *caritas,* the root of the English words *caring* and *charity.*

It could be hard to live with a saint. In another poem, "Soliloquy From the Spanish Cloister," Browning wrote from the viewpoint of a monk who cannot stand one of the other monks living in the same abbey. Virtue can be a challenge to live with every day. However, it is clear in this poem that what is intolerable for the duke is not just that this sweet-faced, good-natured girl appreciates everything around her, but that she does not reserve any special attention for him. She blushes at a compliment from the monk artist making her portrait, not only at her husband. She appreciates everything as much as she appreciates him.

The duke could not tolerate this general appreciation, for he had a jealous form of love, a possessive love. The duke is speaking of his "last duchess" as he speaks of his other beautiful possessions, which he keeps shut away in halls and out of sight of other people. This kind of love is jealous and grasping. It is the antithesis of the kind of love that he describes his duchess as showing. Her natural warmth and pleasure shows for so many people and things around her; it is displayed like a sunset. By contrast, the duke wanted to possess his wife's feelings as he possessed her body and money. He shows jealousy more appropriate to a husband whose wife has broken her marriage vows.

It is significant that as the monologue unfolds, the duchess's painting is kept behind a curtain that only the duke is allowed to draw back. Now he is able to control the display of her smiles. And she smiles only for him.

In an interview, Browning said, "I meant that the commands were that she should be put to death . . . Or he might have had her shut up in a convent."[2] Those were the kind of orders that a nobleman in medieval times might have given, long before the duke was born, if his wife had been unfaithful. There is no hint here of actual infidelity, only that the duke resents her treating everyone with the same kind of caring attention she has for him. He thinks he deserves more.

The duke displays the third kind of love shown in the poem: self-love. The duke's pride and vanity is a form of self-love that is not giving and appreciative, but grasping as he acquires things and tries to control them. The duke's greed is also ineffective in many ways; he is not effective at controlling his wife except to stop all smiles. His efforts to hire artists and build a palace are a tasteless jumble of unconnected artworks.

For instance, he commissioned a bronze sculpture, which would have been very expensive, without knowing how to tell if it was a unique original or one of many copies the artist had made. The duke, after all, hired an artist to paint his wife's portrait but allotted only one day for the sitting and had her wrapped up in a cloak. Small wonder the artist said that her mantle covered her wrist too much.

Historical Background

Browning prefaced the poem with the word Ferrara, to show that the speaker is Alfonso II d'Este, the fifth Duke of Ferrara (1533–1598). At the age of twenty-five, the young duke married Lucrezia di Cosimo de' Medici, daughter of the Grand Duke of Tuscany. She was fourteen, and like many women of the time, not well educated. The Medici family could be considered "nouveau riche" (newly rich) when compared to the distinguished d'Este family. The duke's remark regarding his gift of a "nine-hundred-years-old name" is meant to show that he considered his young wife to be of a much lower social status. What she brought to their marriage was a sizeable dowry. The wedding took place in 1558, but within a few days, the duke abandoned her and his fine house for two years. When Lucrezia died at the age of seventeen, there was a strong suspicion that she had been poisoned.

Promptly, the duke then sought to marry Barbara, the eighth daughter of the Holy Roman Emperor Ferdinand I and Anna of Bohemia and Hungary. Barbara's brother, Ferdinand II, the Count of Tyrol, negotiated to arrange the marriage. Presumably, the person the duke is addressing in the poem is the courier for the count. Other characters named in the poem are fictional, both the monk and painter Frà Pandolf and sculptor Claus of Innsbruck.

Enjambment

The duke's words flow on, uninterrupted. The poem is in rhyming couplets, but he does not end his phrases at the end of lines. He bulls ahead, finishing his sentences where he pleases. The verbs are frequently enjambed—on separate lines from their subjects and/or objects. Starting in the second line, Browning writes:

> . . . I call
> That piece a wonder, now: Frà Pandolf's hands
> Worked busily a day, and there she stands.

In these lines, Browning first separates a subject and verb ("I call") from the verb's object ("that piece"), and then separates a subject ("Fra Pandolf's hands") from its verb ("worked").

By this use of enjambment, the poet is showing readers how to hear the poem, or how to read it aloud. The reader is being shown a duke who speaks at his own speed and says what he wants. What do rhyming couplets matter to a duke? This character will not pause at the end of each line and let the words seem settled and fitted together.

There is a curious and distinct difference in the use of enjambment between this poem by Browning and "Sonnet XLII" by his wife, Elizabeth Barrett Browning. In her sonnet, Barrett uses enjambment in the final lines to draw attention to the last statement her narrator makes. By contrast, Browning uses enjambment in almost every couplet. The effect is that his narrator seems to be saying "Listen to this!" repeatedly. This effect of rushing and calling for attention is particularly strong in the following lines:

> ... and if she let
> Herself be lessoned so, nor plainly set
> Her wits to yours, forsooth, and made excuse,
> —E'en then would be some stooping; and I choose
> Never to stoop. . . .

The duke's speech patterns resist finishing his statements inside the natural line breaks and end rhyme. But "resistance is useless," as author Douglas Adams said.[3] The structure of poetry imposes end rhymes on these couplets; it keeps the duke in line with the rules, even when he does not seem to know how to meet them with grace.

Creating Characters

In this poem only one character is speaking, the duke, and yet somehow it is not a monologue like the soliloquies by Hamlet in Shakespeare's famous play. This poem is not made up only of the thoughts of one character speaking to him or herself. There are other characters evoked as the duke's statements rush along. Through the lines spoken by the duke, the poet is able to give an impression of the other players in the story without any of them being present.

The clearest portrayal, of course, is that of the duke, as he is allowed to speak for himself. A more vague and shadowy figure is the person whom he is addressing, who apparently does not have any opportunities to get a word in edgewise as the duke never pauses to allow natural conversation. This person can be understood to be someone whom the duke feels to be capable of appreciating beautiful art objects but who is only a messenger for the count. The use of the phrase "the Count, your master," is a reminder that the duke is addressing a servant who is not the social equal of either the count or the duke.

The painter Frà Pandolf is actually quoted by the duke. The rhyme in his words "Paint must never hope to reproduce the faint" lets the reader know that he is more of a natural poet and artist than the duke is. However, Pandolf is also a busy worker who gave good value when hired as a painter. By mentioning the other artist, Claus of Innsbruck, the duke looks like a clumsy name-dropper trying to emphasize his own status as a patron of the arts.

The speaker describes the dead duchess more by her reactions to good things around her than by any physical qualities or actions, except for smiles and blushes. As scanty as the duke's description is of her, she is still a character that he cannot control.

The poet never once steps out of the duke's voice to tell the reader who these people actually are or tell the unvarnished truth. The point is for the reader to hear the story from a particular point of view. The duke's rushed portrayals of artists, wife, his foolish retinue of hangers-on, and the count, all say less about those people than about himself: he is a frustrated control freak who is less worthy of a nine-hundred-year-old name than he thinks he is. The poet is more capable and creative than he might appear at first, as his power to imply meaning becomes apparent only after the reader has inferred his message.

Further Study Questions

1. Can you find any examples of repeated vowels, or assonance, in "My Last Duchess"?

2. Why is the portrait kept behind a closed curtain?

3. How do you read aloud the dashes in these lines of poetry?

4. How is the lingering envy of Italian culture still evident in this English poem written in 1842?

5. What signs of humor or comic intent can you find in the poem? While the duke is deadly serious, is the poet as grim as his narrator?

"The Lover and the Syringa Bush" Herman Melville (1819–1891)

I t may seem odd to think of the author of the massive novels *Typee* and *Moby Dick* writing love poetry. But it is true. The published works of Herman Melville include poems on love. Although Melville wrote long novels that were filled with details and explanations of what he was intending the readers to understand, including an entire chapter of *Moby Dick* that was an essay on the symbolism and meaning of white, his poems were brief and almost curt in comparison.

During the 1840s and 1850s, Melville had many connections to the literary circles of New York and the New England states. He kept up correspondence with several writers and publishers and managed to earn a living as a

Herman Melville

The Lover and the Syringa Bush

Like a lit-up Christmas tree,
Like a grotto* pranked* with spars*,
Like white coral in green sea,
Like night's sky of endless stars,
To me, like these, you show, Syringa,
What heightening power has love, believe,
While here at Eden's gate I linger,
Love's tryst* to keep with truant Eve.

***grotto:** cave

***pranked:** decorated

***spars:** breakable, shining minerals

***tryst:** a planned meeting for lovers

novelist. His poetry was of less interest to readers than his other writing, but Melville did not let that stop him from working at his verses in the later years of his life. He had no illusions about changing the world with his poetry. "Of all human events, perhaps, the publication of a first volume of verse is the most insignificant," wrote Melville to his brother in 1860, "but though a matter of no moment to the world, it is still of some concern to the author."[1]

Imagery

In this love poem, the narrator is waiting in a garden to meet with his darling. He addresses a fragrant, blooming bush because it shows him that love has increased his ability to perceive wonders.

There are images used in this poem that some readers might not understand. Syringa is not a syringe or needle—it is the name in Latin for a type of large, hardy shrub with showy and fragrant clumps of small flowers. The name is derived from the Greek *surinx,* for a shepherd's pipe, because the hollow stems can be used to make pipes. There are many varieties in the Syringa species; two of the most common and beautiful of these small trees are called, in English, the mock orange (with white flowers) and the lilac (with purple or white flowers). The strong scent of these flowers is popular for women's perfume. This bush could be a metaphor for a sacred mystery, such as the burning bush that appeared to Moses in the Bible's book of *Exodus,* or the Golden Bough in mythic studies. It could also be a metaphor for a woman's body—scented, fertile, and beautiful.

The expression "grotto pranked with spars" is a fancy way to describe a cave that is not merely a narrow, rough hole but a great underground room decorated with natural rock forms. The minerals could be banded agates and other shiny rock crystals, or they could be shapes in limestone flows that form one drip at a time, such as stalactites and stalagmites (conical cave formations that slowly grow from the cave floor and ceiling). The use of the word "prank" for "decorate" was already old and obscure when Melville wrote this verse. Similarly, "spar" had already come to mean a stout wooden pole, such as a spear or mast, rather than a sparkling pillar in a natural cave. Melville chose archaic words to give some timeless grandeur to his short and simple verse.

He is also using images as reference to places that are distant from this meeting in a New England garden. Coral from the Mediterranean Sea is usually red. By naming white coral, Melville is referencing his travels to the Atlantic Ocean and distant places his beloved will not have seen. Eden was the garden in the first chapters of *Genesis* in the Bible, where Adam and Eve lived before the Fall.

The love described in this poem seems to be an impersonal love of beauty in the natural world, even though the speaker in the poem is a lover waiting to meet with the woman he loves. "Just as art endows Man with a love of beauty, love endows Man with a magical imagination that can transform the world," wrote scholar Laurie Robertson-Lorant. She notes that the poem's narrator waits for his darling "beside a flowering bush so brilliant that its branches seem to hold the sky and sea."[2]

Feeling the Rhythm

Though this poem is brief—only eight short lines with four stressed syllables each—there is still an opportunity for the poet to make a subtle change in the rhythm of the lines. In the first quatrain, or set of four lines, the pattern of stressed and unstressed syllables makes four trochaic measures per line. However, the last trochee is cut short without an unstressed syllable.

In the second quatrain, the pattern of stressed and unstressed syllables is slightly different: here the lines have four iambic feet, so they start with an unstressed syllable. The change in stresses marks the change from the four listed items in the first quatrain to the statement of what the listed items are like. The rhyme scheme of these eight lines is *abab cdcd*, a pattern seen in many songs. However, with four stresses in every line, this poem is not in ballad measure and so cannot be sung to the tune of ballads such as "Barbara Allen."

Perspective

Melville wrote "The Lover and the Syringa Bush" late in life, long after his famous novels *Typee* and *Moby Dick,* as part of a collection of poetry that is known as his rose poems. "Like Picasso's late drawings of the Minotaur," according to Laurie Robertson-Lorant, "Melville's rose poems express a resurgence of eroticism."[3] The narrators in these poems are male, combining elements of religious figures, such as Buddha, Dionysus, and the Gnostic Jesus. Eve in these poems resembles Gaia and Rhea, the Greek earth goddesses before the time of Olympus, where Hera ruled with Zeus.

For decades, there were unresolved contradictions warring in Melville's nature. At times in his youth, he was uncertain about his religious faith. How could he be a good Protestant Christian if he understood why pagans worship nature gods? He also struggled with his feelings of sexual attraction for women and for men because in his youth, he was not wealthy enough to afford to get married, and homosexuality was considered a crime.

It was only late in his life that he was able, by reaching deep inside himself, to find some way to reconcile his own masculine and feminine sides and both the pagan and the puritan within him. This poem shows some of that reconciliation. It seems that like the narrator in this poem, Melville had learned patience and to let love come to him where he waited, ready for it.

Unequal Tone

In this poem, the tone is interesting. The lovers are not peers. The man and woman are not equal complements, joining to be one perfect whole. That's not unusual in traditional love poetry, but usually the poet is the one insisting that he is too lowborn to be worthy of the noble woman who inspires him. That's not the case here.

The unequal nature of their relationship is shown in two ways. First, the narrator is waiting upon his lady's pleasure; he will have to be as patient as he can, waiting until she arrives. When she will eventually show up for their meeting is entirely up to her. While he is admiring the stars and the garden, she is lingering out of sight at the ball or dance instead of rushing outdoors to meet him.

In the last line of the poem, the narrator refers to his love as "truant Eve" as if this woman is a schoolgirl being taught lessons in love by the narrator. He is her schoolmaster, and she is late for a lesson. It now becomes clear why he is waiting in the garden, instead of going to find her. It seems likely that he is an older man who has learned patience, and she is a very young woman who has just learned the power she has to manipulate men and make them wait for her. Their unequal relationship might one day become a marriage, but it is not a partnership of equals.

Who Is Eve?

The narrator's beloved is not given her own name, but is called only Eve, mother of all humanity. Perhaps for him she is beautiful in a general way, or a transcendent way, but not in a personal way that lends itself to descriptions of her qualities. Certainly, the speaker in the poem can admire beauty in several forms, yet somehow the form of the beloved goes undescribed—a curious omission.

This Eve may be late for her date, but the narrator is not calling for her nor speaking to her. Neither does he make an appeal to God or the angels in heaven to bring her to him. Instead, he addresses a flowering tree. Does he write his poem to this tree, likening it to the natural wonders of the world, because he knows he will get no answer from the tree? He has had no answer from his beloved yet. It is possible to consider this poem a work expressing reverence for animism because the narrator addresses the bush by its genus name in Latin for its *genius loci,* or animating spirit.

Because the references to a young woman are less descriptive than the images of the Syringa and other natural wonders, the reader should consider whether the speaker in the poem might not be waiting for a particular girl at all. He might simply be walking in the garden, ready to fall in love, and able to appreciate the beauty that he has already seen but not have met the woman of his dreams.

Further Study Questions

1. Is the narrator of the poem unhappy to be in the garden instead of in the house?

2. What references can you find to religion—Christian or pagan—in this poem?

3. To what tunes could you sing this poem to without it sounding completely silly or wrong?

4. Is the speaker in the poem waiting at Eden's gate on his way into Eden or on his way out of it?

5. What do you think it means that the narrator in this poem is addressing a flowering bush instead of his beloved or his God?

"I Sing the Body Electric"
Walt Whitman
(1819–1892)

Growing up, Walt Whitman educated himself by reading the Bible and the works of Homer and Dante, as well as Shakespeare and other English poets. From the age of twelve, he began work in the printing trade, and then at seventeen he began teaching in one-room schoolhouses on Long Island. By 1841, at age twenty-one, Whitman took up journalism, editing several newspapers in Brooklyn and Long Island in New York. He spent a few months as the editor of the *New Orleans Crescent* in 1848, attending the slave markets in that southern city. This experience deeply marked him and inspired important sections in his poem "I Sing the Body Electric."

Like the other poems in *Leaves of Grass*, Whitman wrote "I Sing the Body Electric" after

Walt Whitman

reading an 1843 essay by the celebrated American writer Ralph Waldo Emerson, in which Emerson expressed a need for the United States to have its own unique poet to write about the vices and virtues of this new country. This poem in particular was Whitman's answer to that call.

Summary

This long poem has nine sections with two excerpted in this book. In it, the narrator is declaring his love for humanity and the human body in all its forms. The first section praises bodies filled with the clean energy of the soul.

The second section states that it is impossible to describe the love of the body, but that people express themselves with the way their bodies move, and the narrator moves among them.

The remaining sections, not shown in this book, continue in the same vein. The third section describes a particularly wonderful man. In the fourth section, the narrator marvels that it is pleasant to be near people. The female body is praised in section five, while section six praises the male body and states that laborers and immigrants are equal with wealthy people. The seventh and eighth sections praise the bodies of a man and a woman being sold at a slave auction, stating that the same passions run in everyone and that love is the same for everybody. The final section states that bodies are poems, lists body parts, and insists that these body parts are parts of the soul.

Excerpt From
I Sing the Body Electric

1

I sing the body electric,
The armies of those I love engirth* me and I engirth
    them,
They will not let me off till I go with them, respond to
    them,
And discorrupt* them, and charge them full with the
    charge of the soul.

Was it doubted that those who corrupt their own bodies
    conceal themselves?
And if those who defile the living are as bad as they who
    defile the dead?
And if the body does not do fully as much as the soul?
And if the body were not the soul, what is the soul?

2

The love of the body of man or woman balks account*,
    the body itself balks account,
That of the male is perfect, and that of the female is
    perfect.

The expression of the face balks account,
But the expression of a well-made man appears not only
    in his face,

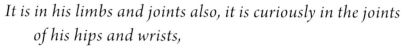

It is in his limbs and joints also, it is curiously in the joints
of his hips and wrists,

It is in his walk, the carriage of his neck, the flex of his waist
and knees, dress does not hide him,

The strong sweet quality he has strikes through the cotton
and broadcloth,

To see him pass conveys as much as the best poem, perhaps
more,

You linger to see his back, and the back of his neck and
shoulder-side.

The sprawl and fulness of babes, the bosoms and heads of
women, the folds of their dress, their style as we pass in
the street, the contour of their shape downwards,

The swimmer naked in the swimming-bath, seen as he
swims through the transparent green-shine, or lies with
his face up and rolls silently to and from the heave of
the water,

The bending forward and backward of rowers in row-boats,
the horse-man in his saddle,

Girls, mothers, house-keepers, in all their performances,

The group of laborers seated at noon-time with their open
dinner-kettles, and their wives waiting,

The female soothing a child, the farmer's daughter in the
garden or cow-yard,

The young fellow hosing corn, the sleigh-driver driving his
six horses through the crowd,

The wrestle of wrestlers, two apprentice-boys, quite grown,
  lusty, good-natured, native-born, out on the vacant lot
  at sundown after work,
The coats and caps thrown down, the embrace of love and
  resistance,
The upper-hold and under-hold, the hair rumpled over
  and blinding the eyes;
The march of firemen in their own costumes, the play of
  masculine muscle through clean-setting trowsers and
  waist-straps,
The slow return from the fire, the pause when the bell
  strikes suddenly again, and the listening on the alert,
The natural, perfect, varied attitudes, the bent head, the
  curv'd neck and the counting;
Such-like I love—I loosen myself, pass freely, am at the
  mother's breast with the little child,
Swim with the swimmers, wrestle with wrestlers, march in
  line with the firemen, and pause, listen, count.

*engirth: encircle, or go round the body like a belt

*discorrupt: heal and make clean

*balks account: cannot be described

In "I Sing the Body Electric," as in most of the poems in his collection *Leaves of Grass*, Walt Whitman's style of writing is a written imitation of some of the qualities of ordinary language, spoken casually. The effect of his phrasing is to make his lines very pronounceable. The phrasing is fluid, allowing a steady stream of words to be read aloud.

There were complaints by contemporary literary critics, quoted in the Academy of American Poets' "Guide to Walt Whitman's *Leaves of Grass*" that "Whitman's free verse didn't fit into the existing British model of poetry, which was a tradition of rhyme, meter and structure." Though the lines in this poem are not strictly metered or rhymed, there are sections of iambic meter, closely mimicking patterns of natural speech and pleasing to the ear.

What one would call paragraphs in a prose story are strophes here, not stanzas with a repeating pattern of rhymes but verses without any repeating patterns of rhyme. The strophes feel natural and improvised rather than straitjacketed into a rigid rhyme scheme. One of the results of this unstructured style is that the poem feels like a spontaneous declaration of love rather than a labored, formal statement. At first glance, the reader might think that this work is prose rather than poetry. A second look might leave the reader wondering whether this poem is disordered and sloppy, or simply unfinished. It might take reading a few lines aloud to see that the words are chosen for their sounds as well as their meaning, and that the lines are crafted not only to be easy to say but to have words with positive feelings associated with them.

The poet was trying with this poem to write a grand celebration of what it meant to be alive and well at that time in a new and growing country. By starting with the words, "I sing the body electric," Whitman is invoking the reader to remember the Roman poet Virgil and other Roman and Greek classic works. Virgil was a formative poet of the Roman Empire who began his epic poem, *The Aeneid,* with the words, "Arms and the man I sing. . . ." Writing in iambic hexameter (lines with six iambic feet) in imitation of the Greek poet Homer, Virgil also borrowed characters and themes liberally from Homer's epic *The Iliad* to make up a history for how the city of Rome was founded. As Whitman references Virgil, he, too, is writing the story of his people in the early years since their founding as a nation; he is trying to become the poet for America that Emerson said was needed.

A striking literary device that Whitman used in this poem is anaphora, or the repetition of a first word in each phrase; for example, a series of lines will begin with "and." By using anaphora, Whitman is mimicking the syntax used in English translations of the Bible. This kind of syntax would be familiar to his readers in the last half of the nineteenth century, when the Bible was the most commonly owned book in American households. Even people who could not read would have heard sections of the Bible read aloud in church services. Anaphora gives some of the lines in this long poem a repetitive, heavy, and substantial feeling like that in an epic poem from the Roman and Greek classics. It also creates hypnotic rhythms.

This heavy return to the start of each line is also present in long lists and catalogs that occur in several places in the poem. In these catalogs, Whitman indicates the broad variety among types of people or marvels at the anatomy of the body. One literary commentator in the "Guide to Walt Whitman's *Leaves of Grass*" wrote: "Whitman's mastery of the catalog has caused critics to praise his endless generative powers" and "his seeming ability to cycle through hundreds of images while avoiding repetition and producing astounding variety and newness." The most striking use of anaphora and catalogs in secular English poetry was by Christopher Smart in part of his poem "Jubilate Agno," where Smart praises his cat. It is very likely that Whitman read Smart's poetry, as he read many works by English poets.

Transcendentalist Movement

Part of the reason that Emerson approved of *Leaves of Grass* was that for him it was a way to revive the transcendentalist movement in American literature. In the 1830s and 1840s in the eastern region of the United States, the philosophical movement of transcendentalism was developed as a protest to the general state of culture and society and, in particular, the state of intellectualism at Harvard University and the Unitarian doctrine taught at the Harvard Divinity School. Among the transcendentalists' core beliefs was the inherent goodness of both people and nature. Transcendentalists believed that society and its institutions of organized religion and political parties corrupted the purity of the individual. Emerson praised *Leaves of Grass* on its first release, and his supporting letter, which called the book "the most extraordinary piece of wit and wisdom America has yet contributed," helped to launch the success of Whitman's collection of poems.[1] Subsequent editions showed changes and new poems in response to Emerson's comments.

Author Theodore Sturgeon was moved by reading *Leaves of Grass*. He wrote: "Outside of Whitman's 'I Sing the Body Electric,' I know of no more exquisite and moving passage than 'The Irish Girl's Lament,'" which Sturgeon included in his story " . . . And My Fear Is Great . . . "

Sturgeon also paraphrased comments in an essay by W. B. Yeats, saying that Yeats "decried artifice and artificiality in poetry, and said that the best poetry, the real poetry, came from the lips and hearts of the people, speaking in their own idiom."[2]

Yeats went on to say about Whitman's verses in particular that when he "writes in seeming defiance of tradition, he needs tradition for protection, for the butcher and the baker and the candlestick-maker grow merry over him when they meet his work by chance." Yeats felt that such people were like "little boys in the street [who] mock at strangely-dressed people." Defending unconventional poems by Whitman, Yeats stated "...somewhere in the heart that they have been sung in temples, in ladies' chambers, and quiver with a recognition our nerves have been shaped to by a thousand emotions."[3]

Impact on Readers

The poem "I Sing the Body Electric" first appeared in Walt Whitman's *Leaves of Grass*, a collection of poems "notable for its frank delight in and praise of the senses, during a time when such candid displays were considered immoral. Where much previous poetry, especially English, relied on symbolism, allegory, and meditation on the religious and spiritual, *Leaves of Grass* exalted the body and the material world," wrote scholar Annie Coleman in her "*Leaves of Grass* Summary."

"Reactions to Whitman have been at both extremes: His book has been banned for sensuality one decade, and then praised as the cornerstone of American poetics the next," according to a recent literary commentator as quoted in the "Guide to Walt Whitman's *Leaves of Grass*." "America's poets and critics have found unmediated love for our most American poet, the man who came to shape our ideas of nationhood, democracy, and freedom."

"I Sing the Body Electric" is sensual, yet in these descriptions of touching another person's body, the references are simple touching of hands or an arm around the neck. Even when referring to sexual love, Whitman does not use foul language to describe intimacy. Even so, some reviewers denounced his poetry, and this poem in particular, as pornographic.

It's hard for a reader in the twenty-first century to be certain whether Whitman's contemporaries were more alarmed by his using the word "love-flesh" or by his impassioned, extended, and repeated insistence that all human bodies were sacred, including both men and women, and specifically the bodies of slaves and recent downtrodden immigrants. In polite society in nineteenth-century America, one simply did not display emotions so publicly. Certainly, this poem is less pornographic than several of John Donne's secular love poems, such as "To His Mistress Going to Bed," "The Ecstasie," or "The Flea."

The first edition of *Leaves of Grass* earned mixed reviews. One reviewer considered the anonymous author to be a loafer, defiant and insolent, while other reviewers thought the work was an odd attempt to revive transcendentalism. When President Lincoln—Whitman's hero—read a copy and praised it, Whitman was no longer shy about putting his name on the cover for the second edition.

For the 1860 edition, Emerson urged Whitman to tone down his poems' sexual imagery. That wasn't enough to help Whitman keep the government clerking job he had managed

Electric Image

In this poem, Whitman's use of the word "electric" does not mean that the body is an unfeeling robot made of wires and tools. Whitman is using this word to describe the vitality of the body, alive with intention and motion. He is also referring to scientific experiments that took place in the eighteenth and nineteenth centuries.

In 1786, the Italian scientist Luigi Galvan published his discovery about how a frog's leg could be made to jump even after the frog was dead, if the frog's body was hanging from a brass hook and the scientist used an iron knife to dissect it. The vital fluids of the body—the blood, lymph, and nerves of the frog—would react to the metals and move. Galvani called this phenomenon "animal electricity."

Another scientist, Alessandro Volta, believed that the electricity was not stored in the animal flesh but happened when the metals were connected by the salty fluids of the body. Between 1790 and 1860, Volta and other scientists built several versions of batteries to generate electricity. By referencing these scientific discoveries, Whitman is showing his awe for learning all the wonders and secrets of the body. He is also showing that he is not a dreamer who scorns science but an observer who feels like Galvan when he admires the vitality of human bodies.

to get in Washington, D.C. James Harlan, Secretary of the Interior, who was offended by *Leaves of Grass*, fired him.

In early 1882, the New England Society for the Suppression of Vice pressured Boston's district attorney, Oliver Stevens, into writing to Whitman's publisher. Calling *Leaves of Grass* obscene literature, Stevens demanded the removal of several poems, including "I Sing the Body Electric." When Whitman refused to censor the new edition, the publisher returned the printer's plates to Whitman and abandoned the project.

For the 1882 edition, Whitman found a new publisher, who believed, like him, that the controversy would increase sales. It proved true. Though many bookstores banned it, the first print run of this edition sold out in under a day. The edition sold out five printings of one thousand copies each.

Whitman's Hymn

The love Whitman describes in this poem is *caritas*. The English word *charity* can seem like a pale, watered-down kind of love after the fire of *eros*, the lasting family bond of *filias*, or the religious fervor of *agape*. Charity has a negative connotation for some people, who think it focuses on the economic differences between those who give and receive, or separates people into categories like "worthy to receive" and "worthy because of giving." As if the worth of human needs or kindness could be counted like cans of condensed milk on a shelf! What Whitman counts in the lists of this poem, and marvels at, are ways that human bodies are alike and have similar feelings.

Put like that, charity does not seem like something which separates people into worthy givers and worthy receivers— and nothing for the unworthy. Charity begins to seem more like caring, the other form of this word in English. Caring for one another can have the connotation of caring for someone's needs, as a nurse tends a patient.

At this point, it is important to note that Whitman was a volunteer nurse during and after the Civil War, spending so much of his time volunteering with patients that it was hard for him to earn an income. Caring can also mean liking a person and taking an interest in her or his well-being. When Whitman writes of love, that pale, watered-down kind of love called *caritas* seems as good as bread.

Without the selectiveness of *agape, filias,* or *eros,* what is love? Is love something you can feel for anyone? If it isn't a unique connection, is it love? In "I Sing the Body Electric," Whitman says that it is. This poem is a hymn to the love of one's fellow man, a love that though vague and impersonal, is broad and deep. Though *caritas* cannot bring the personal pleasures of family, friends, and faith, it brings companionship.

Further Study Questions

1. Based on the vocabulary of the poem, what can you guess about the kinds of work experiences Whitman had before writing this poem?

2. What clues can you find in the poem to tell who the poet expected would be his readers?

3. Choose a few lines of the poem that are appropriate to read aloud. How do the words sound to you? Should they be read in a rushed and hurried way, slow and contemplative, or something different?

4. When the poet addresses the reader directly, does it feel to you as though Whitman is trying to speak to a future reader more than 150 years after he wrote the poem? How is it different to read a poem that seems to be talking directly to readers?

5. Compare a section of this poem with a soliloquy from Shakespeare's play *Hamlet*. How do the lines written by Whitman remind you of Shakespeare's lines written in blank verse? How are the rhythms of stressed syllables similar?

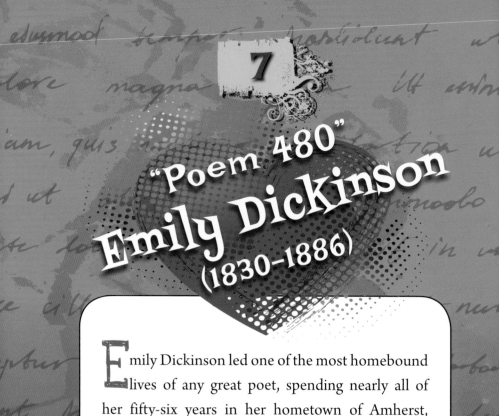

7

"Poem 480"
Emily Dickinson
(1830–1886)

Emily Dickinson led one of the most homebound lives of any great poet, spending nearly all of her fifty-six years in her hometown of Amherst, Massachusetts, and most of those years in the home where she was born and died. The great events of the nineteenth century in America, from the Civil War to President Abraham Lincoln's assassination, play almost no role in her poetry.

Dickinson developed an aphoristic style, using forceful iambic meter disrupted by dashes and imprecise rhymes. Because she was almost unknown as a writer before the posthumous release of her works, critics have not always known what to make of Dickinson's poetic legacy. The conclusion among scholars is that Dickinson ranks with Walt Whitman as one of the two finest

American poets of the nineteenth century, defining an era that had little measurable impact on her poems.

Dickinson actually never read the works of Whitman, her contemporary, on the advice of others who assured her his poems were disgraceful. Among her influences were the Reverend Charles Wadsworth, Henry Wadsworth Longfellow, the Bible's book of *Revelations,* and the Metaphysical poets of seventeenth-century England: John Keats, Robert Browning, and Elizabeth Barrett Browning. She knew the works of the transcendentalist writers in Concord but did not consider herself one of them.

Emily Dickinson

Poem 480
("Why Do I Love" You, Sir?)

"Why do I love" You, Sir?
Because—
The Wind does not require the Grass
To answer—Wherefore when He pass
She cannot keep Her place.

Because He knows—and
Do not You—
And We know not—
Enough for Us
The Wisdom it be so—

The Lightning—never asked an Eye
Wherefore it shut—when He was by—
Because He knows it cannot speak—
And reasons not contained—
—Of Talk—
There be—preferred by Daintier Folk—

The Sunrise—Sire—compelleth Me—
Because He's Sunrise—and I see—
Therefore—Then—
I love Thee—

Summary

The speaker in this poem explains that she cannot keep her place when her beloved is near because of her unspoken affection for him. The speaker and her beloved do not need to speak to answer each other. They cannot speak because of what society will say about them. The beloved forced her to love him because when he arrives, it is as if she is suddenly able to see.

The first line of the poem is punctuated oddly. It seems that the speaker in the poem is quoting a question that has been put to her. Perhaps the text is her attempt to answer that question. It is not significant that she addresses the listener as "You" rather than you; all of the pronouns are capitalized in the poem.

The poem's speaker is speaking to her beloved, saying that she cannot help but love him; it is automatic and as natural as grass bending in the wind or an eye blinking shut when a lightning bolt flares brightly. When the sun rises, there is light and she can see. Her love feels as involuntary as being able to see the sunrise. Just as the grass responds to the natural laws of physics by bending in a gust of wind, so she responds to her beloved.

Although her beloved has a higher status—which she holds in awe—she is still able to chide him by reminding him that the wind never demanded that the grass answer when he called. Lightning never asked a dazzled eye to explain why it blinked because he knows an eye cannot speak. This reproach is as gentle as the woman of Canaan's reply to Jesus in Matthew 15:27. When Jesus answered her request for help by saying that it was not right to take the children's food and throw it to dogs, she said humbly, true, but dogs eat crumbs that fall from the table. Through the poet's images, the speaker in Dickinson's poem is saying that her beloved is like a grand and awesome power of nature, like wind, lightning, or a sunrise, while she is as plain and inarticulate as grass. She does not compare herself to a mouth, but to an eye, meaning that she can see her beloved but is incapable of explaining her response to him.

This response is heartfelt. She is drawn to him and cannot keep still when he goes by, like grass that bends in the wind. If the wind knows not to make demands of the grass, doesn't her beloved understand? There are things people *just don't* talk about.

Dash Away

This poem's almost incoherent jumble of phrases is a good example of what the narrator means when she likens herself to things that cannot speak. The ideas seem fragmentary; or at least, there is no complete sentence in this poem. There are brief phrases and sentence fragments tacked together by dashes, not even commas or colons.

In punctuation, there are rules for what parts of a sentence can be connected by using a comma or a colon, but dashes are a different matter. Using a dash means that one set of words or a sentence fragment can be followed by another with a different subject entirely. There are no real rules. A statement can start and abruptly change to a question, an interjection, or an observation. Two people could be finishing each other's sentences, and the sentences might end differently from how they began.

Using dashes in the way that Dickinson does can reproduce some of the ways that many people actually do speak, in sentence fragments and unconnected sets of words. There is no steady rhythm of stressed syllables that would allow this poem to be sung to a ballad in common measure. At least there is one thing clear from the way the short lines are set on the page: if the poet intends the reader to pause at the end of a line, there is punctuation to indicate that pause, such as a dash or a question mark.

This poem was one of nearly eighteen hundred found among Dickinson's papers after her death. Her literary executors were her friends and poets themselves, familiar with the dozen or so poems that Dickinson had seen published during her lifetime. When organizing her poetry notebooks for posthumous publication, her friends edited several of the earlier poems for the first two volumes, replacing her unconventional use of capital letters and dashes with more conventional punctuation for easier reading. "Poem 480" was published in a later volume, less edited than the first volume, and more true to Dickinson's handwritten notebooks.

Triplet Verses

Of the more popular writers of love poetry, Dickinson has been heavily edited. However, this poem is one that escaped the influence of her editors. There is no way to be certain how Dickinson's editors would have laid out the poem numbered 480 if they had edited it as they had changed her earlier poems. But there are striking differences between this poem and some others in her notebooks. Among them is the possibility that she did not intend to write this poem in common measure, or ballad form, with the standard rhythms of many of her poems. There is a joke among English Literature students, which says that it is possible to sing any of Emily Dickinson's poems to the tune of "The Yellow Rose of Texas." While that tune certainly can be used for her poem numbered 712 or "Because I could not stop for Death" (and the result sounds bizarrely inappropriate), it is not possible for this poem.

It is possible that the first lines composed of "Poem 480" were not the lines at the top of the page but the images in three sets of three lines. Certainly, these images are the most polished and coherent and evoke the clearest images for a reader's mind. Readers can only guess whether these images were the clearest for the writer as well.

The first set of three lines has either a rhymed couplet and a following line or three end rhymes with a slant rhyme for the last line that uses the same final consonant, *s*, with a differing vowel before it:

> *The Wind does not require the Grass*
> *To answer—Wherefore when He pass*
> *She cannot keep Her place*

The second set of three lines suggests the pattern should be read as a rhymed couplet with an unrhymed line following:

> *The Lightning—never asked an Eye*
> *Wherefore it shut—when He was by—*
> *Because He knows it cannot speak—*

The final set of lines splits the third line into two parts but laid out here as three rhyming lines would read:

> *The Sunrise—Sire—compelleth Me—*
> *Because He's Sunrise—and I see—*
> *Therefore—Then—I love Thee—*

If a Japanese poet had composed this as a haiku, it might have been written as three short verses of three lines each; however, end rhyme is not a feature of Japanese poetry. While Dickinson was a knowledgeable reader in her day, Japanese poetry was not popular among English readers. It is entertaining to pick these triplet verses out of the poem and speculate about whether the poet was experimenting with short forms.

Who Do You Love?

There are many ways to dissect this poem, but there are two common interpretations. The first discusses the poem as a realistic description of Dickinson's love for someone she could not marry. Some Dickinson biographers have suggested that she found herself unexpectedly in love with a Massachusetts Supreme Court judge in a nearby town, but the match was not suitable. Society would not accept it because of the difference in age and station between Dickinson and the judge. The poem's narrator addressing the beloved as "Sir" and by the reference to "Daintier Folk" seems to support this idea.

The other interpretation suggests that the poem describes Dickinson's love for God, even though she was at odds with the church and the unforgiving religion she was taught as a child. As the narrator of the poem addresses her beloved as "Sire," this opinion makes sense. In her teens, there was a Christian revival in her hometown; she felt the pull but came to resist and distrust orthodox attitudes.

As an adult, she read a great deal and took to spending hours outdoors on her father's land, walking over hills near her home and finding reverence in nature. She wrote several other poems expressing her religious feelings, which were positive, sustaining, and surprising to her after learning as a child to fear hellfire and damnation.

Homebody

Emily Dickinson was born in Amherst, Massachusetts, and died there in her family home fifty-six years later. "There is no better example of the New England tendency to moral revelry than this last pale Indian-summer flower of Puritanism," wrote literary historian Norman Foerster. "[H]er place in American letters will be inconspicuous but secure."[1]

According to Foerster and other biographers, in modern terms, Dickinson would be considered agoraphobic. People with this anxiety problem are unable to leave home because they fear having panic attacks. Years went by without Dickinson leaving the house, and many more years in which she would walk no farther than the fence around her father's grounds. Yet once a year she would invite in a houseful of guests, including all the neighbors, and be the perfect host at this open house. Well acquainted with everyone in her village, Dickinson corresponded regularly with a few friends who were poets, such as Thomas Wentworth Higginson and Helen Hunt Jackson. As her literary executors, these friends published most of Dickinson's poetry posthumously.

When Dickinson wrote about loving God, to scholar Roland Hagenbuchle, she was showing her Neoplatonic beliefs about perceiving the true nature of the universe by seeing it in distorted reflections in the natural world. "The finite self's desire for the divine Other is in the nature of things," Hagenbuchle wrote. "Whereas [philosopher] Kierkegaard found the Other in the saviour figure of the Biblical God, Dickinson, at odds with religious orthodoxy, was thrown back on the evidence of the soul's desire for the missing Other."[2]

The Romantic poets had faith in the creative potential of the self but were particularly aware of its precarious status. They were disturbed by the idea that for each of us, the self is separate from its transcendental origin with the Divine; the Romantics felt alienated, as though free will was not effective. "With Emily Dickinson, this sense of alienation is raised to a new pitch," according to Hagenbuchle. "Dickinson's cultural heritage—especially the paradoxical nature of Puritan selfhood along with the Transcendentalist emphasis on 'Self-Reliance'—radicalized the problem for her, and she was forced to look for new tactics in her effort to reconstruct a viable New-England self."

Further Study Questions

1. What impact does rhyme have in this poem, where there is no repeated pattern of rhyme?

2. How is a dash different from a comma?

3. Is this poem the words of one speaker or two? How can the reader tell? What can you find to support the idea of one speaker or two?

4. When reading this poem aloud, how are the dashes to be used? Are they all short pauses, long ones, or are they pauses of differing lengths?

5. How would this poem look if another famous poet used this poem as a first draft? Choose a poem by another poet, such as Elizabeth Barrett Browning or Richard Brautigan, and try rewriting "Poem 480" so that it looks like the other poem. What changes have you made?

"Colored Toys" Rabindranath Tagore (1861–1941)

Rabindranath Tagore was born the youngest of a large and wealthy Bengali family in Calcutta, India. His parents were Brahmins of Hindu faith, social reformers who made their house a cultural center. Learning at home with a series of teachers, young Rabindranath read many classic works of literature and modern science. At sixteen, his first published poetry, short stories, and dramas began appearing under a pseudonym, including his translation of Shakespeare's *Macbeth* into verse in the Bengali language.

As the manager of family estates in what is now Bangladesh, Tagore kept aware of the lives of the common people and increased his interest in social reforms. He founded a school in 1901, a year before his beloved wife died, and the school was a great comfort to him in his grief. During this time, Tagore wrote a great deal and modernized Bengali literature by composing in modern forms, such as short stories and free verse, as well as classical Indian forms.

In 1921, Tagore expanded his school into Viswabharati University and endowed it with all the royalties from his books and the prize money from his 1913 Nobel Prize. As a scholar, Tagore had the confidence to debate with Albert Einstein and maintained lasting friendships with Mahatma Gandhi and Jawaharlal Nehru. As an activist poet and author, Tagore was the natural choice to compose the national anthems of India and of Bangladesh. Bengalis still sing his songs.

Rabindranath Tagore

Colored Toys

When I bring to you colored toys, my child,
I understand why there is such a play of colors on clouds,
    on water,
and why flowers are painted in tints
—when I give colored toys to you, my child.

When I sing to make you dance
I truly know why there is music in leaves,
and why waves send their chorus of voices to the heart of
    the listening earth
—when I sing to make you dance.

When I bring sweet things to your greedy hands
I know why there is honey in the cup of the flowers
and why fruits are secretly filled with sweet juice
—when I bring sweet things to your greedy hands.

When I kiss your face to make you smile, my darling,
I surely understand what pleasure streams from the sky in
    morning light,
and what delight that is that is which the summer breeze
    brings to my body
—when I kiss you to make you smile.

Summary

The speaker in this poem is a parent who learns how to understand good things about being alive in the world by giving good experiences to his or her child.

Tagore has put all his talent to describing not the grand love of patriotism but the personal love of a parent for a child. Each of these four verses has strong sensory images to evoke things that the narrator has seen, heard, tasted, and touched.

There is no verse for the sense of smell. Scent and taste are often combined in some languages, especially when describing food, as Tagore does in the third verse. There are other possible reasons for not having another verse about scents; the poet might not have had a strong sense of smell or might not have known how to cook or make perfumes and other good scents. In addition, the mention of flowers in the first and third verses implies their scent as well as their appearance. Tagore is able, even when writing in a language not his own, to use words that have more than one purpose for making imagery from the senses.

The song's format is much like a ballad format—four short lines that make up each verse, each with a completed thought. This song form of verses is common not only in English but in other languages around the world. In "Colored Toys," however, the number of stressed syllables per line is not constant, and the words do not follow a metrical pattern.

In each verse, the narrator states that when he gives something to his child, such as colored toys, music, sweets, and kisses, he understands why there are similarly good things in the world. The colors in clouds, water, and flowers are understandable when he gives colored toys to the child. The poet uses the words "a play of colors" and says, "flowers are painted in tints." The word "play" is an active word—a noun naming the action done when the colors are actively being moved on clouds and water. Also, the word "painted" implies that the flowers have been painted by a painter acting to put dyes on the flowers. Are colors in the world like toys that are given to everyone?

In each verse, the poet makes similar word choices. The verbs that the poet uses imply that the pretty colors are painted, the pleasant sounds dance, the fruits have been filled with sweetness, the sunlight brings pleasant warmth, and breezes bring delightful coolness. As the narrator tells the story, he makes good experiences for his child, and now he understands the good experiences all around him in the world.

Do leaves and waves dance to make music for the world, just as the narrator sings for the child? Are flowers and fruits gifts like the sweets the narrator gives the child? Could sunshine and summer breezes be like a parent's kisses? If so, is there a giver who gave these gifts?

In Other Words

This poem appeared in the first of Tagore's books published in English, *Gitanjali*. This title is a new word invented by Tagore, combining the Bengali words for "song" and "offering." Originally, Tagore wrote the poems in Bengali and then translated them into English. "Colored Toys" has been recorded as a song many times and listeners around the world have enjoyed it, even if they did not know the poem was first written in Bengali.

No translator was hired to convert this poem from Bengali into English. Tagore composed the translation himself. Gradually during his long life, he translated most of his published works from Bengali into English. At first, the effect a translator can have on the original concepts of a poem might not be obvious to readers. When translating poetry from Chinese into English, for example, some Chinese words need to be translated into a phrase instead of an English word because the languages are organized so differently. Fortunately for Tagore, Bengali and English have similarities because both came from the ancient Proto-Indo-European language, from which most languages in Europe and part of Asia are descended. In poetry, there are also subtle intentions and suggestions that might not appear in a translation because the translated word might not have the same associations in the other language. The Italians have a saying: *tradutore, traditore,* which means "the translator is a traitor."

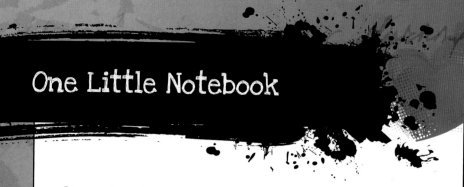

One Little Notebook

One Little Notebook

In 1912, during Tagore's second visit to England, he looked for something to do. On the long sea voyage, he began translating his latest poems into English in a small notebook. His son left the notebook in a briefcase on the London subway. Luckily, the briefcase was recovered. When painter William Rothenstein, Tagore's only friend in England, heard of this notebook, he encouraged Tagore to let him read the poems.

As an admirer of Bengali and Indian writings in translation, Rothenstein could see the worth in the poems. He brought the notebook to the attention of his friend, W. B. Yeats. The poems enchanted Yeats, who was a famous and influential poet. Arranging for the book's publication, Yeats even wrote the introduction. Tagore had already begun to enjoy success in his home country, but with this book's release in September 1912, he became an overnight international sensation at age fifty-one, first in British literary circles and later on speaking tours worldwide.

Tagore toured many countries, giving talks on multiculturalism, diversity, and tolerance, and fund-raising for the university he founded. "Tagore had early success as a writer in his native Bengal," scholar Horst Frenz said. "For the world he became the voice of India's spiritual heritage; and for India, especially for Bengal, he became a great living institution."[1] In 1913, Tagore became the first non-European to be awarded the Nobel Prize for Literature.

In English, this poem is in simple language. The words are short and easy to say. The vocabulary is simple and uncomplicated, like basic English. Because of translation, the word selection for sounds through assonance and consonance are much simpler in the English version than in the original Bengali.

Tagore's goal was not to fit his poem into a rhyme scheme, a traditional Bengali style, or a European pattern for rhyme, such as a sonnet or villanelle (a French poem form with entire lines repeating according to a pattern). Instead of a formal poetic style, Tagore translated his free verse poem into a similar free verse style with no regular rhythm patterns and no end rhymes. Each line is a complete phrase or sentence, with its subject, verb, and object all written in that word order. Every phrase is all on a single line without enjambment, which would place the subject and object of a verb on separate lines. By building lines that are complete phrases, the poet makes each verse seem orderly, structured, and finished, even though there is no rhyme scheme or rhythm pattern.

Further Study Questions

1. How does the poet evoke sensory images in the reader? Does he use adjectives, such as "sweet," or other parts of speech?

2. Based on the poem, what can the reader guess about the poet's beliefs in religion and the origins of the world?

3. How does the poet tell the reader that this child is well, healthy, and active, not a newborn or badly disabled? What images does the poet use?

4. What makes the love featured in this poem the love of a father for his growing child, instead of the love that a mother has for her baby? What clues are in the choice of words?

5. Compare one of the verses in "Colored Toys" with the first four lines in "My Last Duchess" by Robert Browning. How does enjambment affect the way you read both sets of lines? How does the arrangement of complete sentences on the lines of these poems make you think differently about how the narrators in these poems are speaking?

Note: Questions that ask for reader opinions will vary. There is no one correct answer. Responses should, however, demonstrate a close reading of texts.

CHAPTER 1: "Westron Wynde" Anonymous

1. While love poetry is usually considered to be written by a man about his love for a woman, it's possible for a reader to find reasons in this poem to support the narrator being either a woman or a man.

2. Traditional anonymous songs do not have copyright. Composers can use them for inspiration without stealing. Listeners and reviewers will know about the traditional song and not be fooled into thinking the new song is completely original.

3. Answers will vary according to the student's interests and experience. The verse written should be able to be sung to one of the same tunes that "Westron Wynde" could use.

4. Answers will vary. The student could describe a strong opinion or perhaps explain why the identity of the poet doesn't matter.

5. Answers will vary. Some students will be familiar with other music based on traditional tunes. Students who like playing or composing music might enjoy improvising on a traditional tune or writing formal music for a small performance.

CHAPTER 2: "Sonnet 130"
William Shakespeare (1564–1616)

1. The volta occurs in the thirteenth line with the words "And yet, by heaven, I think my love as rare." Arguably, the word "yet" is enough by itself to signal that there is a change in the focus. Alternatively, the entire line is needed to show how this statement is different from all the preceding statements about the beloved.

2. The narrator loves to hear his mistress speak. Since music has a more pleasing sound than her voice, it can be guessed that he loves to hear what she has to say rather than just the sound of her speaking.

3. Among the reasons for mentioning heaven could be that the poet wishes to make his love for the Dark Lady seem holy. He could be showing a spiritual side after so many images that are physical, describing his beloved's appearance. A cynical answer is that the three syllables of "by heaven" were needed to fill out the rhythm of the line.

4. Answers will vary, but will probably say that the description is more realistic than idealized. It would be interesting to see and compare drawings of the Dark Lady.

5. Answers will vary. One difference between a hinge word in a haiku and a volta is that the Japanese word is very likely to be about an element of nature or one of the seasons, where a volta does not have that restriction.

CHAPTER 3: "How Do I Love Thee?"
Elizabeth Barrett Browning (1806–1861)

1. The use of anaphora is made more interesting by having the rest of each line contain strongly contrasting images, which describe simple or complicated emotions in a few words or many using variably structured sentences.

2. It was a Victorian convention that the word "Men" as used in this line can be taken to mean "adult humans" or "persons" and not specifically adult males.

3. There are many possible answers, but the narrator speaks as if her childhood were long in the past, and as though she has been an adult striving for right and meeting daily needs for some time now.

4. Answers may vary, but a possible answer could be that the speaker seems to be proud of having feelings for the beloved and capable of expressing these feelings properly. The speaker seems modest because she is not demanding anything, nor is she saying that she deserves anything from either the beloved or God.

5. Answers will vary. People have differing ideas of how to present male or female characters. The speaker in this poem has known great joy and strives to do right even though she has been frustrated in the past. Some readers assume, as Petrarch did, that the normal state for a poet and his narrator is to be male and that the female beloved is a higher being who does not have human failings.

CHAPTER 4: "My Last Duchess"
Robert Browning (1812–1889)

1. There are several examples of assonance in most of the couplets, where the vowel sound in the end rhyme appears elsewhere in the couplet, often in the second line and again in the last word of the line. In the first couplet, the vowel sound in "wall" appears in "alive" and in "call."

2. The painting is kept behind a curtain, which only the duke draws aside, so that now he is the only person who can reveal her smile.

3. There are several ways to read the dashes in these lines. Perhaps the reader will pause or hesitate longer than for a comma. Another way to read the dashes is with a shift in tone or speed. Some readers pause briefly and make a gesture, trying to show the change in the character's thought process.

4. Several answers are possible. Readers might consult books about the Renaissance in England and Italy or articles about the increasing popularity of Shakespeare's poetry during Victorian times in England.

5. Answers will vary. The poet seems to have made the narrator of the poem look rather foolish as he speaks in a rush without waiting for his companion to contribute to the conversation. The narrator also looks foolish when he brings up the death of his first wife while negotiating a marriage contract for a future wife. Also, he seems to talk about each art object in his collection as he comes to it, with the attention span of a butterfly.

CHAPTER 5: "The Lover and the Syringa Bush"
Herman Melville (1819–1891)

1. The narrator seems happy enough for the moment, looking at the beautiful bush and remembering wonders he has seen in the past.

2. There are at least three overt references to Christianity: the Christmas tree in the first line, Eden's gate in the seventh line, and Eve as the last word of the poem. There are perhaps seven references to other faiths. The Christmas tree was borrowed from pagan and Norse beliefs in Germany. Grottoes or holy caves in Europe were used for religious ceremonies for thousands of years before Christians built altars in a few of them. Coral has been carved into pagan fetishes as well as beads for Catholic rosaries. Some animists believe that the sea, sky, and stars are all alive and holy, and so is the Syringa bush.

3. There are four stressed syllables in every line of this poem. The tunes of some church hymns ("Joyful, Joyful, We Adore Thee" or "Shall We Gather at the River") will work with these words because hymns commonly have four stresses per line and allow an extra unstressed syllable here and there. Because this poem is not written in common measure, the tunes of most ballads and many popular songs ("Barbara Allen" or "House of the Rising Sun") will not work with these words.

4. Answers will vary. The reader could answer either that the narrator is waiting to leave the garden with his beloved or to return to the Garden of Innocence with his Eve.

5. Answers will vary, but it is possible the reader might feel the narrator addresses the bush because he feels that he's more likely to get an answer from the bush than from either his God or his darling.

CHAPTER 6: "I Sing the Body Electric" Walt Whitman (1819–1892)

1. Answers will vary, but they might include firefighting, fishing, shooting, newspaper writing, studying, swimming, nursing, or other medical work.

2. Based on the narrator's comments about slaves and immigrant laborers, it seems that the poet expected that the readers would be people who were more prosperous than a slave or a new immigrant, perhaps working folk who might read a book occasionally.

3. Answers will vary, but the descriptions could include any of the following adjectives: enthusiastic, proud, cheerful, pleasant, old-fashioned, or confident.

4. Answers will vary, but the reader might have more to say about the poet's effort to speak directly to the reader than about his success at speaking to readers in the twenty-first century.

5. Answers will vary, but the reader should be able to find a set of lines from this poem to compare with a set of lines from *Hamlet*. There will be comments to make about iambic lines sounding like natural speech, about

no regular rhyme scheme in either set of lines, and about the poets' efforts to try to write like the thoughts of the narrators.

CHAPTER 7: "Poem 480"
Emily Dickinson (1830–1886)

1. Some readers feel that any rhyme in this poem seems accidental. For others, the few end rhymes have more impact because they are rare. Other word choices for consonance or assonance may matter more here than rhyme.

2. A comma is a pause at the end of a phrase or between items in a list. A dash may come at any point in a line of poetry—often a point where another punctuation mark could be used, but sometimes it is used to splice together a few words with no connection.

3. While it is possible to argue that there are two speakers in this poem, most of the evidence supports the idea of one speaker.

4. Answers will vary, but the reader should be able to give some reason for each answer, even if the answer is only that it sounds right to pause in a certain way.

5. Answers will vary. If this poem is rewritten in the style of American poet Richard Brautigan, one likely change is that there will be phrases with subjects, verbs, and objects even though the punctuation will still be unconventional, as in his writing in "Watermelon Sugar." If a poem by Elizabeth Barrett Browning is selected, the lines will have

conventional grammar and punctuation. If this poem is rewritten in the style of Shakespeare, it might become a sonnet.

CHAPTER 8: "Colored Toys"
Rabindranath Tagore (1861–1941)

1. There are many descriptive words used in this poem, such as "color" rather than red or blue, or "flower" rather than jasmine or rose, to suggest and evoke images in the reader's mind rather than detailing exactly what colors the reader is supposed to imagine. It is possible that using a noun or a verb instead of an adjective makes a more subtle image or engages the reader more in thinking.

2. Answers will vary. Based on the poem, it can be guessed that the poet is implying that the natural world is not a soulless place, empty of intent, which only accidentally happens to have qualities that are pleasant for humans. It is possible to argue that the poet believes in a creator God who has given these qualities for the benefit of all creation. It is also possible to argue that the poet believes that each part of the natural world is intentionally making itself a gift for the benefit of fellow beings.

3. Answers will vary, but the images suggest that the speaker is talking to a child who can see and hear, as well as play with toys, eat, and dance—not a tiny newborn who drinks only milk.

4. Answers will vary. The poem is certainly compatible with the love of any parent for a child. Because the images do not suggest that the parent is a mother giving birth to or

breastfeeding her child, it can be argued that the poet meant to refer to the kind of parental love felt by fathers and adoptive parents.

5. Answers will vary. It's possible that by having complete phrases on a single line, the narrator in "Colored Toys" seems to have collected his thoughts before speaking, while the enjambment used by the narrator in "My Last Duchess" makes him seem distractible.

Chapter Notes

INTRODUCTION

1. Percy Hornstein, *Reader's Companion to World Literature* (New York: Brown Mentor/Penguin Group, 1981), p. 548.

2. John Donne, "Elegy XX: To His Mistress Going to Bed," in *Poems of John Donne, vol. 1* (London, Lawrence & Bullen, 1896), pp. 148–150.

3. Dick Jensen, "Ruminations," *Spaced Out Inc.*, n.d., <http://spacedoutinc.org/DU-16/WorldWellLost.html> (October 10, 2012).

CHAPTER 1: "Westron Wynde" Anonymous

1. Markfromireland, "Sunday Playlist: Taverner 'Westron Wynde,'" *Saturday Chorale*, October 9, 2011, <http://saturdaychorale.com/2011/10/09/sunday-playlist-taverner-westron-wynde/> (October 21, 2012).

2. Marisa Fox, "Music Review: MCMXC a.D," *Entertainment Weekly*, No. 57, March 15, 1991.

CHAPTER 2: "Sonnet 130" William Shakespeare (1564-1616)

1. Sarah Milligan, "Sonnets and the Sickroom: The Invalid Persona in Elizabeth Barrett Browning's *Sonnets From the Portuguese*," MA essay, University of Victoria, 2012, p. 24.

2. Percy Hornstein, *Reader's Companion to World Literature* (New York: Brown Mentor/Penguin Group, 1981), p. 548.

3. Milligan, p. 24.

4. Michael Best, "The Sonnets: The Cast of Characters," *Internet Shakespeare Editions*, April 1, 2011, <http:// internetshakespeare.uvic.ca/Library/SLT/life/youth/ sonnets2.html> (April 8, 2013).

5. Herman Melville, "Letter to Evert Duyckinck, March 3 1849—Melville's Reflections," *The Life and Works of Herman Melville*, Multiverse, July 5, 2000, <http://www.melville.org/hmquotes.htm> (September 4, 2012).

CHAPTER 3: "How Do I Love Thee?" Elizabeth Barrett Browning (1806-1861)

1. Sarah Milligan, "Sonnets and the Sickroom: The Invalid Persona in Elizabeth Barrett Browning's *Sonnets From the Portuguese*," MA essay, University of Victoria, 2012.

2. Jennifer Kingma Wall, "Love and Marriage: How Biographical Interpretation Affected the Reception of Elizabeth Barrett Browning's *Sonnets From the Portuguese* (1850)," *Victorian Web*, May 4, 2005, <http://www.victorianweb.org/authors/ebb/wall1. html> (November 12, 2012).

CHAPTER 4: "My Last Duchess" Robert Browning (1812-1889)

1. Sarah Milligan, "Sonnets and the Sickroom: The Invalid Persona in Elizabeth Barrett Browning's *Sonnets From the Portuguese*," MA essay, University of Victoria, 2012.

2. William Harmon and C. Hugh Holman, *A Handbook to Literature, 8th edition* (Upper Saddle River, N.J.: Prentice Hall, 1999).

3. Douglas Adams, *The Hitchhiker's Guide to the Galaxy*. BBC Radio 4, March 15, 1978.

CHAPTER 5: "The Lover and the Syringa Bush" Herman Melville (1819-1891)

1. Herman Melville, "Letter to his brother Allan, May 22 1860—Melville's Reflections," *The Life and Works of Herman Melville*, Multiverse, July 5, 2000, <http://www.melville.org/hmquotes.htm> (September 4, 2012).

2. Laurie Robertson-Lorant, *Melville: A Biography* (Amherst, Mass.: University of Massachusetts Press, 1998), p. 612.

3. Ibid.

CHAPTER 6: "I Sing the Body Electric" Walt Whitman (1819-1892)

1. James E. Miller, Jr., *Walt Whitman* (New York: Twayne Publishers, Inc., 1962), p. 27.

2. Theodore Sturgeon, "Story Notes," *A Saucer of Loneliness: Volume VII The Complete Stories of Theodore Sturgeon* (Berkeley, Calif.: North Atlantic Books, 2000).

3. W. B. Yeats, "What Is Popular Poetry?" *The Collected Works of W. B. Yeats, Vol. IV Early Essays* (London: Simon and Schuster, 2007), p. 9.

CHAPTER 7: "Poem 480" Emily Dickinson (1830-1886)

1. Norman Foerster, "Emily Dickinson," Ward & Trent, et al, *The Cambridge History of English and American Literature* (New York: G. P. Putnam's Sons, 1907–1921; New York: Bartleby.com, 2000).

2. Roland Hagenbuchle, "Sumptuous—Despair: The Function of Desire in Emily Dickinson's Poetry," *The Emily Dickinson Journal,* Vol. 5, No. 2, Fall 1996, pp. 1–9, <http://muse.jhu.edu/journals/edj/summary/v005/5.2.hagenbuchle.html> (September 4, 2012).

CHAPTER 8: "Colored Toys" Rabindranath Tagore (1861-1941)

1. Horst Frenz, Nobel Lectures, Literature 1901–1967 (Amsterdam: Elsevier Publishing, 1969), Nobel Prize. org, n.d., <http://nobelprize.org/nobel_prizes/literature/laureates/1913/tagore-bio.html> (January 23, 2013).

Glossary

accent—Emphasis given to a syllable of a word in ordinary speech.

alliteration—Repetition of the same initial sound of words.

anaphora—Repetition of the same first word in several phrases in a row.

animism—A doctrine that the vital principle of organic development is immaterial spirit.

aphoristic—Tending to write or speak in tersely phrased statements of a truth or opinion.

apostrophe—Speaking to someone absent or dead, or to something nonhuman, as though it were alive and present and able to hear and reply.

assonance—Repetition of the same vowel sound in nearby words, to harmonious effect.

blank verse—Lines written in unrhymed iambic pentameter.

cantus firmus—The steady chant in a mass written in four parts.

common measure—Lines written in ballad format.

consonance—Repetition of the same consonant sound in nearby words.

couplet—A pair of lines that rhyme.

enjambment—When the verb of one phrase is on a different line from either its subject or its object.

foot—A repeating pattern of stressed and unstressed syllables, also called meter.

free verse—Poetry written without a strict meter pattern.

metaphor—A symbolic comparison or representation used in literature to convey additional meaning by relating an object or concept to something that is already known.

Puritan—A member of a sixteenth- and seventeenth-century Protestant group in England and New England opposing as unscriptural the ceremonial worship and the prelacy of the Church of England.

rhyme—Recurrence of similar sounds in words, especially the last syllable of a line.

Romantic poets—(1790–1860) Poets who linked nature to human emotions, seeking in nature a deeper connection to humanity.

secular—An adjective describing attitudes or activities with no religious or spiritual basis.

slant rhyme—Words that share some but not all vowel or consonant sounds.

sonnet—A poem of fourteen lines, usually in one of two rhyme schemes: Italian or Petrarchan sonnets are rhymed *abbaabba cdecde* with an octave of eight lines followed by a sestet of six lines; Elizabethan or Shakespearian sonnets are rhymed *abab cdcd efef gg.*

stanza—A group of lines within a poem whose meter and rhyme scheme follow a pattern that is exactly repeated.

strophe—A group of lines forming a separate part of a longer poem that is in blank verse or with no regular pattern.

volta—The pivot point or turning point of a sonnet, usually at or near the beginning of the sestet in Petrarchan sonnets.

Further Reading

Books

Andronik, Catherine M. *Wildly Romantic: The English Romantic Poets—The Mad, the Bad, the Dangerous.* New York: Henry Holt and Co., 2007.

Franco, Betsy, ed. *Falling Hard: 100 Love Poems by Teenagers.* Cambridge, Mass.: Candlewick Press, 2008.

Pockell, Leslie, ed. *100 Essential American Poems.* New York: Thomas Dunne Books, 2009.

Soto, Gary. *Partly Cloudy: Poems of Love and Longing.* Boston: Harcourt, 2009.

Internet Addresses

The Poetry Foundation: Love Poems
<http://www.poetryfoundation.org/love-poems>

Poets.org: Love Poems
<http://www.poets.org/viewmedia.php/prmMID/5860>

Index